the
word
on
coaching

the word on coaching

Words to Live, Lead, and Coach By

JoAnn Auger,
Kevin Fuselier,
and Debby Neely

Tandem Light Press

950 Herrington Rd.

Suite C128

Lawrenceville, GA 30044

Tandem Light Press paperback

ISBN: 978-1-7376438-0-7

PRINTED IN THE UNITED STATES OF AMERICA

CONTENTS

Foreword Xi

Acknowledgments Xiii

Introduction. Xvii

How to use this Book. Xxi

Accountability 1

Acknowledgment 7

Barriers. 13

Change 19

Coach. 27

Culture. 35

Curiosity 41

Discovery. 49

Emotions & Emotional Intelligence. 57

Environment 67

Expectations. 75

Feedback 81

Focus 89

Goals & Goal Setting. 97

Habits 105

Integrity. 111

Intention 117

Judgment 123

Language 129

Listen. 137

Messaging. 143

Mindset 151

Presence 159

Questions 165

Relationships 173

Resistance 179

Safety 187

Silence 195

Time 201

Trust 207

The Last Word 213

References 215

Resources 217

Journal 219

About the Authors 225

To my family, who are my biggest supporters, loudest cheerleaders, and most robust encouragers to achieve my dreams. You remind me what is really important in life.

-D.N.

To my loving wife, Teresa, and our wonderful children—Jackson (Hailie), Giselle, Warren, and Evonne, for their enduring support as I pursue my dreams. Thanks for believing in me and reminding me that with God all things are possible.

-K.F.

For my son and daughter, Mason and April, and their spouses Janna and Paul, all of whom said stop talking about it and do it. I did it

- J.A.

*The growth and development of people is
the highest calling of leadership.*

—Harvey S. Firestone

FOREWORD

In essence, coaching skills are life skills: and those are skills that Debby, JoAnn, and Kevin have in spades. Reading this book, you will learn many of those skills from these three exceptionally talented and experienced leadership coaches. They have "been there and done that" in a variety of challenging leadership roles through their careers, and they've won over many unbelievers along the way. As a result, their credentials for writing this book are exemplary.

As a passionate practitioner, master coach, and facilitator myself, I have met and trained new coaches in sixteen countries on five continents. When I first met the authors almost twenty years ago, I knew I was meeting three people who were already making a difference—and they still had so much to offer. They picked up coaching initiatives and ran with them, then came back wanting more—more resources, more knowledge, more training. In fact, more of anything that would equip them to meet their goal: to put coaching in the hands of leaders in their large, successful, and demanding organization. They had (and still have) fire in their bellies and a dream to bring coaching skills to everyone.

The Word on Coaching is a handy distillation of how the authors have used their knowledge and skills to support and inspire busy managers. You can open this book anywhere and start reading. I particularly like the way Debby, JoAnn, and Kevin have written each section using their personal experience, and the firsthand stories they use to demonstrate their skills in action.

Although this book is crammed with valuable insights from cover to cover, first make sure you read *Coach* (and not just because I got a mention). This chapter will establish what coaching is and what it is not. Follow that with *Feedback*, *Presence*, and *Questions*. By then, I guarantee you'll be hooked and will read and reread the whole book because it is so useful, practical, and inspiring.

Cheryl Smith,
Master Certified Coach

ACKNOWLEDGMENTS

We are extremely grateful for the learning, encouragement, support, and love we have been given along the way of this journey of writing a book.

It is often said that you don't know what you don't know. No words have ever been truer than when we set out to write this book. Thank goodness Caroline Smith and Tandem Light Press came into our lives. This book would not have been published without your knowledge and advice, which was always given with care, empathy, and humor.

Debby

To my friends who told me that I should write a book, who always asked how the book writing was going and gave an uplifting word, who kept telling me how cool it will be to have a book with my name on it, and who I know will be the first ones in line to buy the book, I cannot thank you enough for being part of my "tribe." I will always support you and your dreams like you have supported mine.

To the great leaders I have worked with over the years who have modeled what it means to be a leader even during the toughest times, who let me coach them (even when I wasn't very good at it yet), and for supporting me to write a book like this. Keep coaching.

One of the greatest joys of being a coach is the connections you make with other coaches. I have been so fortunate to have strong, caring coaches in my life. I learn from you and appreciate you.

Special acknowledgment to Master Coach Cheryl Smith, who believed in me right from the start and made me the coach I am today.

To JoAnn and Kevin: Three friends sat around a hotel pool one night talking about their passion for coaching and helping leaders, and that has resulted in this book. It has been challenging, inspiring, frustrating, and invigorating all in one. I could not have asked for better coauthors who have prayed, laughed, and commiserated with me. I hold much love and admiration for both of you for the coaches you are and even more for the people you are.

Kevin

First, I want to thank God for his provisional wisdom in placing the people in my life who have given it color and dimension.

I would like to honor my first teachers—my mother (Portia Ford-Tompkins) and my grandmother (Gustavia Ligons-Anderson). They nurtured me, taught me, and lived as examples before me. I am forever grateful for the love they invested in me.

I want to give recognition to my Sunday school teacher, Queen Esther, who taught me the power of a good question.

To my family and friends for listening to me talk about all the things I would like to do. Your listening, encouragement, and coaching have paid off and I owe you one. Some of you I owe more than one.

JoAnn

Wow! We did it. Thank you, Debby and Kevin, for the friendship and tenacity to make this happen. What a journey it has been. I have learned and grown (sometimes, it wasn't pretty) as a coach, friend, and human being. You are the kind of folks that I want to be a part of whatever you do.

To all those leader-coaches who inspired me and taught me, I wish that I could name each of you but know that you are in the words.

A great deal of gratitude goes to Cheryl Smith, master coach. You have always been my role model as a leader-coach and one of my biggest encouragers. If only we could clone you.

Mason, Janna, April, Paul, Sabine, Atlas, and Evander—you are the reasons that I strive to be the best version of myself. Thank you for believing in me and goading me when needed. You are deeply loved.

INTRODUCTION

This book is the culmination of the work of three former colleagues with very different personalities and backgrounds, who live in different states and time zones. Our common ground for doing the hard work of writing this book is our passionate belief in the power of coaching.

The biggest hurdle we faced was defining what we were we going to offer that hasn't been already written or presented. We all struggled with that. Each of us has been in the coaching world for a while. We are experienced leaders, and we are successful coaches. And we say this humbly (but factually): each of us is very good at our craft. This means that you will be able to glean from the collective experience and knowledge of three experts in their field to support you in your journey of being a leader-coach. We have witnessed what can be accomplished when a leader decides to embrace the power of being a leader-coach.

What do we mean by *leader-coach*? Simply put, a leader who moves away from a command-and-control approach and toward a coach approach is a leader-coach. You will learn more about this in the Coach chapter.

The primary reason that we wrote this book is to help good leaders transform into powerful leader-coaches. How we show up to the people we lead is a key factor in how successful we are as leaders.

We all wanted to write a book that leaders at all levels would find beneficial. We talked with numerous leaders about what they needed and what they didn't want in this book. One of the many things that we learned is that leaders do not have time to read a dense, multi-hundred-page book about how to be a leader-coach. They want the takeaways to be straightforward with real-life application. And they want to be able to easily locate a particular topic or skill that they are interested in.

We discuss both employee performance and development coaching in this book. Performance coaching is when you are providing feedback and direction to help people meet performance standards. This focused coaching is assisting people in understanding how they can do more and better work. Using the information and tips in this book, we illustrate to leaders how to use coaching to overcome production problems, performance issues, or relationship hurdles, which hinder performance.

Development coaching is when you see a person on your team who has the potential to move to higher levels of responsibility or higher levels of leadership. Giving feedback and coaching in this context is about helping the person identify their career aspirations, recognize their potential, and supporting them in developing a plan to acquire the knowledge, skills, and abilities they will need to be competitive for current and future opportunities. This type of coaching helps individuals take ownership of their development and have a plan on how to advance their careers.

A lot of thought was given to not only what you might need to succeed but also how you might need it. We have all held leadership positions in corporations and small businesses as well as being informal leaders without the official title. We understand that you need a resource that is easy to read and simple to use, and that supports you in moving to action. In our opinion, the most interesting leadership books include stories, examples, tips, and resources. That is what you will find in this book. You will enhance your knowledge and then have an opportunity to discover how to make what you're learning work for you. You will see results if you take what you learn and use it.

We hope that you will gain insight into the foundational knowledge and skills needed to be an effective and influential leader and coach in your organization. We hope to provoke thoughtfulness and action, spark curiosity, and provide clarity and structure for those individuals who want to be coach-like in their approaches to leadership. We also hope to help any leaders build the foundational knowledge and skills needed to be effective as leaders who are competent in both performance and development coaching in the workplace.

Coaches3 (that's what the three of us call ourselves) took all the feedback from our amazing leader-coaches and have written a practical, relevant, skill-building, and transformative book. We are excited to share our knowledge and experiences alongside friends who are some of the best coaches in the world of leadership.

—Debby, Kevin, and JoAnn

HOW TO USE THIS BOOK

We want to explain how we organized *The Word on Coaching* and suggest ways to use it. Our objective was to keep it simple and straightforward. We did that by selecting specific words that embody and/or help explain what we define as leadership coaching. Once we identified those words, we then narrowed them down to the ones that were most significant and descriptive to being a leader-coach. We wrote a chapter about each word, explaining its importance and connection to being a leader-coach. And because one of us (that person will remain nameless) thought we should put the chapters in alphabetical order, we did that. One could argue that putting the chapters in order of importance for skill building and understanding would be the way to go. We discussed that idea a great deal and finally decided that all the skills are equally important and having a simplistic, straightforward approach would be more beneficial to our readers. Putting the chapters in alphabetical order does make it simpler to locate a specific topic and serve as a "field guide." Each chapter defines the coaching word, gives real-life examples, tips, and skills, and asks reflective questions to support application of the skills and insights. At the end of each chapter, you will find other suggested chapters that will enhance the reader's understanding. In other words, this is not your typical book. So where do you start? Here are our suggestions:

- We believe a good place to start is the Coach chapter. Understanding what we mean by being a leader-coach will give context to all the other chapters.

- This book can be read front to back, or you can pick and choose a chapter that interests you.

  ○ Maybe you are an experienced leader and want to review a few elements of coaching as a refresher or to gain additional insight? Picking a specific word that you want to review or learn more about is one approach.

  ○ Maybe you are new to leadership and coaching? We recommend that you read the chapters alphabetically after you read the Coach chapter.

- You can scan the chapters to see if there is a particular word that catches your attention. Start there.

We highly recommend that you answer the reflection questions at the end of each chapter. That's where the real learning takes place. Be honest. Often leaders fail to take what they have learned and put it into action. They know what they should do, but it never happens. There are many factors/reasons for that—accountability, support of their leadership, how to apply the skills, and so on. We help address that by giving you reflection questions and blank journal pages in the back of the book to capture your thoughts and ideas of how to use the information and create a plan. If you take time to reflect and then create a plan, you will more likely be successful.

- Choose your own journey through the book. You will notice at the end of each chapter we recommend words that you may want to read next. Or pick another word that interests you or just read the next chapter. It is really your choice how you use the book.

- We also believe that this book will be a good resource if you are trying to create a coaching environment. We suggest picking a word to discuss with your team and other leaders. This is a great book for dialogue sessions and learning together.

Now that we've covered how to use this book, let's get started.

ACCOUNTABILITY

*An obligation or willingness to accept
responsibility or to account for one's actions*

—Merriam-Webster.com

Leadership guru Simon Sinek says, "Give someone responsibility and they will do their best. Make them accountable and they will do even better."[1] Leaders often tell us that they struggle with holding others accountable. This is why we believe coaching is so powerful for leaders. Part of the beauty of coaching is that accountability is built into the coaching conversation. A coaching conversation includes gaining clarity, identifying how to move forward, addressing possible barriers, and getting commitment.

Often, later, leaders will admit they also have a hard time holding themselves accountable for having these conversations. If you have the accountability conversation in the very beginning, it can make your job less difficult. And who doesn't want less difficult? Start by stating what you need from them. Solicit their input on how they can make that happen. Discuss what they need to be successful, potential

---

1   Simon Sinek Facebook post, December 02, 2009.

barriers they might encounter and how to deal with those barriers, and the level of commitment they will need to get it done.

When you set expectations up front, providing feedback later is an easier conversation. We've heard leaders say that no one really wants feedback. On the contrary, employees often tell us that they want feedback from their leaders. They don't want their leaders to wait until the situation cannot be rectified. You should be checking in and providing feedback before you have reached the point of no return. Most employees want to do well, and they definitely want to hear if they are doing a good job. They need to hear from their leaders.

Remember to suppress any judgments and offer a safe space. Safety allows people to

- tell you why they were not able to do what they said they were going to do;
- remove barriers they did not think existed before; and
- open up and tell you what is really going on and trust you.

Do not wait to address accountability issues. Waiting too long can damage your credibility and destroy team morale, not to mention put your team behind in getting desired results. It can take a long time to recover. If there is a pattern of not holding others accountable, you might want to do some reflection on how *you* are leading.

Accountability allows success for both you and others.

> **Tips**
>
> **Approach accountability conversations using a coach approach.** When you know it is time to have an accountability conversation, reflect on what you want as an outcome. Embrace the intention to understand what is really happening and the truth of the entire situation. Stay in discovery mode by asking questions, being curious, and not rushing to judgment. There could

be a valid reason why the person did not do what they said they were going to do.

Be open. Sometimes, we assume they did not do something because they did not want to do it or they simply blew it off. When you approach someone, be respectful. Asking "Why didn't you do this?" is not going to get the outcome you desire. Instead, ask questions like "What got in your way of accomplishing this task?" or "What stopped you from achieving this goal?"

Do not assume. It can be easy to get caught up in assumptions or to start telling yourself a story, "Yeah, here they go again. I knew they were not going to do this. They had the same issue last year." It is important when you get into these situations to keep your mind clear and control your judgments. If someone feels they are being judged that person is not going to be able to hear what you have to say. Consider other options on what might have happened to help keep your mind open.

Take care of business. Part of holding others accountable is knowing when it's time for consequences. We have seen even the toughest leaders struggle with knowing when it's time to let someone go. Not everyone is going to be the right fit. Sometimes, people land in the wrong spot. We all remember the first person we had to let go. We truly believe that you can fire someone and have them walk away with their dignity intact.

It's not a time for surprises. It is important that there are no surprises. You should be having accountability conversations about expectations, whether they are meeting those expectations, and offering your support throughout.

Example

I was coaching an employee who was new to their role. As we discussed what they were going to do to meet expectations, I was watching for clues to their level of commitment. I asked questions like the following:

- *What will your responsibility be in this situation?*
- *What are you committed to doing and by when?*
- *What do you see as your role in getting this done?*
- *What might get in your way?*

Since I did not know them well enough yet, I still could not tell how committed they were. So, I asked them on a scale of 1–10, with 10 being highly committed, where they saw themselves and why. This allowed us to have a good conversation about what they were thinking and feeling. I discovered that the employee's confidence in completing the tasks we had discussed was low. I was able to encourage them and provide some resources. Their words to me as they walked away were "I can do this."

When I have employees tell me they are committed to the task and then not accomplish it after we have had the coaching conversation, it is easier to have a follow-up conversation. I can refer to what they said in the earlier conversation and open the door to discuss barriers, consequences, and how to move forward.

—Coach Debby

Reflection Questions

What are some questions that you can use in future accountability conversations?

_____

_____

What opportunities are you missing to have accountability conversations up front?

_____

_____

What will you do to remain open and create a safe atmosphere for these conversations to occur?

_____

_____

What are the clues you can look for to gauge level of commitment?

_____

_____

Take a minute to reflect and assess how you are doing with accountability by answering these questions. Consider asking a colleague or your team for their assessment of how you are doing in these areas. Then capture notes on what you might want to do to make improvements.

- Are you setting clear expectations, or could you be clearer?
- Is your desire to have others like you getting in the way?
- Are you avoiding potential conflict or tough conversations because you do not feel comfortable addressing those issues?
- How consistent are you with holding accountability conversations?

Capture additional thoughts and big ideas in the journal section in the back of the book.

Other related words: Culture, Expectations, Feedback, Goals, Questions, Resistance

ACKNOWLEDGMENT

*To express recognition of a truth, fact or quality
of someone's contribution or existence*

—FreeDictionary.com

There are numerous studies about employee engagement that show the importance of acknowledging people in the workplace. It is a key contributor to retention and productivity. Most of us want to feel valued and appreciated. It is part of our humanness. Acknowledging others lets them know that their efforts are noticed and they are on the right track. It can also help employees identify and maximize their strengths. Acknowledging people builds positive and productive relationships.

What does it mean to acknowledge someone? Real acknowledgment is not the same as a compliment. Compliments can be shallow and generic. Just telling someone they did a "good job" is generic and can sound insincere. Also, acknowledging is not the same as feedback. Feedback is more about behavior and performance (see the Feedback chapter). Feedback can include acknowledgment. Acknowledging is more about the person's character, attributes, and values. So how do you acknowledge?

Tips

Be Specific. Give details of what contributions the person made. Share the skills and insights that were noticed. And explain how they contributed to a positive outcome and how their values, attributes, and character contributed to it. This requires you to be present and observant.

Be Timely. Share the acknowledgment as soon as possible. It will be more relevant and appreciated.

Drop the "I". Remember it's not about you. Using the word "I" puts the emphasis on you. It can sound judging and come across as a power play.

Be Sincere. Acknowledging people should always be authentic. People recognize when you are only checking the box. Be prepared for people to be suspect of your acknowledgment if this has not been a practice of yours. It may take a while for folks to believe that you are being sincere.

Mix it up. Verbal acknowledgments can be powerful because you are using your voice. You are present and looking at the person. It can be an immediate boost to someone's self-esteem and engagement level. A written acknowledgment has value in that it can serve as a reminder to you and them of their value and contribution. There are multiples ways to acknowledge someone. We encourage you to consider who the person is and how they may prefer to be acknowledged. It is important to know how a person likes to be acknowledged. Some prefer it to be private and one to one. Others like group recognition. Remember the purpose of acknowledgment is to encourage and appreciate the person—not make them feel awkward or slighted.

Don't give it and then take it away. When acknowledging someone, avoid minimizing or canceling out the acknowledgment by using the word *but* or immediately giving correction. Example: "Joe, your ability to take complicated steps and simplify them for others has been so helpful to the team, but I would really appreciate it if you would not be too helpful." This is confusing and is devaluing their skill and who they are. Perhaps a better approach would be: "Joe, your ability to take complicated steps and simplify them has been so helpful. It shows your commitment to the team and ensures that the project is successful. I wonder if you would be willing to help me brainstorm ways that we could teach your skill to others?" This approach is much more positive and productive.

Be Consistent. Consistency has direct impact on your success. Studies state that leaders lose credibility if they do not follow through on behavioral changes or promises. People prefer consistency so they know what to expect from their leader. Don't misinterpret people's lack of response (or appreciation) to your acknowledgment as if it doesn't matter or is unnecessary to them. Often, they are skeptical about your sincerity and consistency. Be determined to follow through.

Example

I vividly remember one of my early-career performance reviews. Performance reviews were not on my list of favorite things to do. Most of my experiences were either painful or a waste of time. It was obvious that many of my supervisors didn't like doing them any more than I liked enduring them. This particular performance period, I was reporting to a new supervisor. He was likeable enough and certainly kept our team on our toes. The dreaded performance review time was around the corner, and I received a request from my new supervisor to come prepared to discuss a list of questions that he had written out. Most of the questions were about how I perceived my performance and skills. There were some other questions about what I valued and liked doing, what brought me energy and joy, how I would describe my character.

I was baffled as to why I needed to answer all these questions; he was the supervisor, so he should know the answers to these questions—at least about my performance. After all, that was his job. I admit that I half-heartedly answered most of the questions. My appointed time arrived, and I entered my supervisor's office with little expectation. That meeting became the highlight of not just my day but my year.

I left that day feeling that I had won an award. I actually felt valued. For sure, I received feedback about some things that I did well and things that I needed to improve, and we discussed how I would do that. But that was only part of the discussion. This supervisor also told me how he saw my values at work and how I contributed to the team and the organization's vision and mission. These were not general statements. He had specific examples with specific attributes. He also asked me to share my perspective of my work and contributions. It was a real dialogue. Frankly, it felt good. I found myself wanting to contribute more and learn more. This supervisor didn't just acknowledge me during my performance review. He seemed to make a point to acknowledge me often. And I wasn't the only person; he acknowledged other teammates. He became one of my role models when I decided to move into a leadership role.

—Coach JoAnn

The example above is the story of a leader-coach who understood the importance of acknowledgment. This supervisor made acknowledging his team part of the culture. It is important to note that it doesn't require a chunk of your time to have daily or weekly check-ins with each of your team members. These check-ins could be anywhere from five to thirty minutes and easily include an acknowledgment. As already stated, consistency is key, even if you just do it on a quarterly basis. And remember, to acknowledge someone, you must be present and observant. This doesn't require you to follow them around. But it does require you to be informed, which could include written or verbal updates, input from coworkers, and/or required reports.

Take a look at the following example and see if you can identify what makes it a good acknowledgment: "Thank you for all the hard work that you have put into this project. I observed you yesterday explaining the new procedure to a couple of your teammates who seemed a little frustrated about the new process. You let them talk through their frustrations and then thoughtfully explained the reasoning behind the new procedure. That was really helpful in getting them re-focused. We appreciate having you as part of the team."

Acknowledgment has been proven to be a major component of highly productive and engaged teams. Give it a try.

Reflection Questions

How often do you acknowledge others for their contributions? Are you consistent?

_____

_____

What gets in your way of acknowledging others?

_____

_____

What are some attributes or skills that you have observed in others that should be acknowledged?

_____

_____

What is one thing you are willing to do in the next ten days?

_____

_____

Capture thoughts and big ideas in the journal section in the back of this book.

Other related words: Culture, Feedback, Environment

BARRIERS

*Something that obstructs or impedes
and prevents access or progress*

—FREEDICTIONARY.COM

HAVE YOU HAD this experience? You work with someone to create a plan for something specific to happen. You leave the meeting thinking that the plan was well laid out and executable, only to check back a few days later to find the plan has fallen apart. There are plenty of excuses and reasons given, but not much on how the plan derailed or how to get back on track. What happened? Or perhaps you have experienced this: You plan to do more asking than telling and more listening than directing your employees. You want to show up more as a leader-coach than the primary problem solver. Yet most of those opportunities to coach are ignored or fail. Why?

The two examples just described reflect what we, as coaches, see every day with leaders' best-laid plans. A good plan is created, steps are outlined; it's executable, but it falls apart. Why? We could list several reasons, but in our years of experience (personally and professionally), we believe that oftentimes the most important questions are not asked: What is going to get in the way of this plan happening? What are the barriers, and how do we address them?

Why do we need to discuss barriers? Barriers can exist for the leader-coach and for the person being coached. To successfully coach others, we as leader-coaches must look at our own barriers as well as help others discover their potential barriers.

Talking about potential barriers removes the element of surprise that can immobilize or cause us to be stuck because we didn't see it coming. If we recognize and plan that barriers will occur, we are able to problem solve ahead of time. And the good news is often we can remove that barrier before the plan is executed. Asking people about potential barriers gives people permission to talk about likely barriers as well as other things that may get in the way. These things may be barriers that you as the leader may not see or think about because you view the project/work from your perspective. Discussing barriers can give you insight to the following:

- what type of training may be needed for individuals and/ or the team;
- strengths and challenges of individuals and/or the team;
- how much buy-in individuals or the team have in the project/work; and
- how to prioritize aspects of the project, identify gaps or even re-work the plan.

> ### Tips (for supporting others)
>
> **Where to start.** An important question to ask once the plan or next step has been defined is "What could get in your way of doing this?"
>
> **Pushback.** If the answer is "nothing is going to get in the way," we all know that things do get in our way. Acknowledge their

commitment but ask the question again. Oftentimes, people are reluctant to suggest barriers for fear of showing up as incapable or incompetent or not a team player. And the trust level between you and that person plays an important role in their ability to admit there may be barriers.

Communicate. Have consistent and productive communication. Put a communication plan into action and actually follow it. Allow for honest and open dialogue. This will help identify barriers sooner.

Listen for self-limiting beliefs—Pay attention to assumptions or perceptions that people have about themselves and their abilities. Some things you may hear them say are "I'm not in their league," "I'm not experienced enough," or "I can't do that." Challenge those beliefs and help them identify what beliefs are creating barriers. Once they are identified, support the person in addressing them.

Empower them. Empower and encourage people to problem solve and make yourself available to discuss potential solutions if needed.

Recognize them. Acknowledge and reward your employees for working through the barriers.

Environment matters. Barriers are not the same for each person. Create an environment of trust and transparency that supports individuals in addressing *their* personal barriers. Constant criticism or derogatory language can create additional, deeper barriers.

Tips (for you – the leader-coach)

Everyone has barriers. Recognize and accept that you have barriers as well—barriers to coaching and barriers to working your plan.

Address self-limiting beliefs. As coaches, we make assumptions and have perceptions about our ability and who we are. Ask yourself, "What stories am I telling myself that are keeping me from moving forward?"

Question yourself. One of the most important questions to ask yourself is this: "What will get in my way?" The second question should be "How do I address each of those barriers?"

Implement a strategy. Ask yourself, "What is one thing I could do today to address this barrier?"

Don't always be the problem solver. If you're a strong problem solver, resist telling others what you would do and how you would do it. As leaders, we can take over projects or micromanage if we fear that the project/plan is not going the way we want. We become the barrier. Leaders often think they must be the subject-matter expert (SME). Oftentimes, they got to their leadership positions because they were that SME. Trust us on this one: Asking for your team's input and listening to their insights will bring great rewards!

Take the time. Time is one of the primary barriers that leaders struggle with. Remember that you do have time to coach. It must be a priority just like other important leadership activities. Data shows that when a leader coaches employees, the employees are more productive and become better problem solvers.

Give trust. Trust your employees to do what needs to be done.

Trust yourself. Believe that you can ask the right questions.

Get a coach. Having a coach will help you address your barriers and make you a better coach and leader. If you do not know where to find one, ask around in your network or consult with your leadership or HR.

Example

Early in my coaching career, I was working with a leader who had set as one of his goals to have one-on-one conversations with each of his employees. He laid out his plan and decided it was doable. I asked the obligatory coaching question, "What will get in your way?" His answer was that lots of things could, but he was determined to follow the plan. A couple of weeks later, during our check-in, he stated he was still trying to figure out the time issue. This went on for a few check-ins. He identified the primary barrier as time, but no progress had been made.

After a few more check-ins and not much progress, I asked if we could use the coaching session to discuss his barriers to having his one-on-one conversations with his team. He first resisted by saying that it was just a time issue that he was working on. I asked if we could start with that statement. He agreed. My question to him was "On a scale of 1–10 (10 being the highest), how important is it to you to have the one-on-one conversations?"

He sat with the question for a minute and then answered, "Obviously, not that important." Getting to the real barriers can take time. Often, as coaches, we can see a barrier before the person being coached recognizes it or is willing to admit to it.

—Coach JoAnn

Talking about barriers can give insight about potential obstacles/issues that otherwise could be assumed a nonissue, ignored, or undiscovered. Discussing potential barriers up front could save time, money, and energy later on, and we know how important each of those are to the success of any plan or organization. Lastly, the primary key to identifying and addressing barriers is that the leader-coach must create an environment of openness, trust, and transparency that allows others to be vulnerable and honest.

Reflection Questions

What is getting in your way of using a coach approach with your team?

How can you hold yourself accountable to ask your team about potential barriers in getting the desired outcomes achieved?

What do you need to do to increase your trust level of your team to get the work done? What do you need to see more of or less of to trust your team? What do you need to do more of or less for your team to trust you?

What are two things that you could do to influence the environment that would encourage transparency?

Capture additional thoughts and big ideas in the journal section in the back of the book.

Other related words: Environment, Culture, Time, Trust, Questions

CHANGE

To undergo transformation, transition, or substitution

—Merriam-Webster.com

Sixth-century Greek philosopher Heraclitus once said, *"The only constant in life is change."* Big, small, personal, professional—you will have to deal with all kinds of change, both for yourself and with those you lead. We see a lot of leaders who approach change as if they should be able to communicate the change and everyone will own it, do what needs to be done, and move on. It typically does not work that way.

Everyone deals with change differently. Some people will move from hearing about the change to acceptance quickly, while others may move painfully slow. Emotions about the change abound—fear, uncertainty, discomfort. You may be asked to lead in ambiguity. You may not be privy to all the information or understand the vision. Things may not be figured out even though the change is proceeding. You may be personally affected. Still, you will be asked to step up and lead. It is your job to figure out how to best support yourself and others during times of chaos.

We have actually heard leaders say, "We don't have time for

coaching or developing our employees—we are going through change!"
Actually this is the most important time for both of these things. When
could listening, trusting, and showing empathy be more needed? When
would be a better time for employees to feel at their best? William
Bridges's book *Managing Transitions* tells us to focus on transition, not
just change. What is the difference? Change is something that happens
to people, even if they don't agree with it. Transition is internal. It's
what is happening in people's minds as they go through change. Guess
what? As a leader, you are dealing with both and showing up as a leader-
coach is imperative for the success of all involved.

One of our favorite coaching questions is *What is in your control?*
There may be a lot of things outside of your control. Focus on the
things that you can control. There are more of those than you think.

- **How you communicate.** Communicate clearly and often. Tell
  your team why the change is necessary. Tell them and then tell
  them again. Share what you can, when you can. Feeling like you
  have information to make good choices has a calming effect on
  people. You may have had time to hear information and let it
  settle in. Your team may be hearing it for the first time. Keep
  this in mind when determining how to communicate.

- **Use storytelling.** This is an underused skill that can be
  extremely powerful and effective. Especially during times
  of change when you can share a time you successfully navi-
  gated a change or was a part of a team that became stronger
  by going through a difficult time together. Our stories cast
  an image and convey emotion that allows us to connect
  with others and drive a point home. Sharing our stories can
  influence others to buy-in to an idea, increase productivity,
  change a habit or behavior, and follow a vision.

- **Meet people where they are.** You can do this by asking
  questions, listening, and observing. Try to look at things
  from their perspective.

- **People, not numbers.** Show others that you care about them. Even though things may not turn out the way they want, they can still walk away with dignity for themselves and respect for you. Withhold your judgment.

At some point in your leadership career, you will face resistance to change. It can be easy to resort to your authority, but you can't force someone to support a change. And if you don't deal with it, it can infect your entire team. We are big fans of Dr. Stephen Covey's *The 7 Habits of Highly Effective People*. In this case, Habit 5: Seek First to Understand, Then to Be Understood comes to mind. Spend some time finding out what is going on with this person who is resisting. Are they afraid? Did they have a bad experience with change in the past? Do they trust leadership? Once you have more information, you can decide the best way to support this person in getting unstuck.

Leadership consultant and coach Dana Vogelmeier shares the following advice:

> When people hear about a change, they may experience anger, fear, and frustration. Support them in moving to inquiry, experimentation, and discovery. That is where you start hearing things like "tell me more" and "can we see what it's going to look like?" That is a step closer to acceptance. As a leader, you need to be trained well to listen and address what you are hearing your people say.[2]

When you decide to be a leader-coach, there will be shifts that you need to make. You may need to think, act, and look at things differently. You will no longer be the problem solver. You will need to listen more and ask questions. You will need a foundation of trust that is nonnegotiable with your team. All these changes will not happen overnight. Show yourself and your team some grace and stick with it. Keep your eye on the intention to come out of change stronger and wiser. When all is said and done, adversity makes us better leaders.

---

2   *The Word on Coaching Podcast*, Season 2, Episode 5.

Tips

Resist the urge to micromanage. Unfortunately, during times of change, we often see leaders become micromanagers. The message they are sending out is that they don't trust their employees. You don't want to inadvertently push your good employees out the door.

It's not always a team sport. Handle performance issues individually. Do not punish the entire team for one person's issues.

Acknowledge progress and results. Is your team still getting the job done? Do you see people working hard to support the change? Are employees encouraging each other? Do you appreciate their focus and dedication? Tell them.

Do it now. Don't wait for a big change to work on team culture. Get to know your people. Start today by creating an environment of trust, empowerment, positivity, and teamwork. What makes the people on your team tick? What motivates them? What is important to them? Discover these things now.

Put on your oxygen mask first. Don't forget to take care of yourself.

- Take some time to figure out where you are with the change and how you can move toward acceptance.

- We wouldn't be good coaches if we did not suggest that you would benefit from having a coach.

- Walk the talk. Remember, your team is watching you. Be the calm during the storm of change. Model what you expect from them.

Example

The organization that I worked for was going through a reorganization, and rumor had it that jobs would be relocated and/or reduced. You could feel the anxiety in every meeting, on every call. We had been given a date when we would be told more information about the future and options. I had been through big changes before, and I felt that I could manage this period of change, no matter the outcome. What I underestimated was my brain getting hijacked. It started with unease over the unknown and a feeling of everything being completely out of my control. It was hard to focus and to make sure my customers did not notice anything different in the service they received. It seemed like every conversation with my coworkers turned to people guessing what they thought was going to happen. Business as usual did not seem possible.

What got me through this turbulent time?

- *A leader who always took a few minutes to ask me how I was doing before we talked about work, who made sure I knew that I could ask her anything and call her anytime, and who encouraged me to focus on potential opportunities and not tell myself doom-and-gloom stories. Guess what? I did ask her questions that she did not have the answers to. I did call her when I felt like I was at the end of my rope because I knew she wouldn't judge me. I did feel like she cared about me and what happened to me. She recognized the work I was doing and made sure I knew that I was valued. She did all of this even though leadership was also affected by these changes. She stepped up to be the leader I needed.*

- *A friend who reminded me that I have choices regarding how I make a living, how I serve my purpose, and how I react to things. Remembering that I always have a choice in situations is something that I had been working on. When I acknowledged that I knew I had choices, she asked, "Then why are you acting like you don't?" Bam! There it was. It was the mind shift I needed.*

When the plan was communicated, that information made me feel even more in control, and the anxiety went away. My boss and friend were right there as I processed what I wanted to do and moved forward. By the way, this example involves a big change. What my leader and friend did would work with any change—big or small.

—*Coach Debby*

Reflection Questions

How would you rate yourself on the following skills with 0 being 'needs a lot of work' to 10 being 'I got this'?

- Communication skills   _____
- Storytelling   _____
- Acknowledgment   _____
- Resilience   _____
- Self-compassion   _____

Pick one of these skills to improve. Capture one thing you will do in the next ten days to improve that skill.

_____

_____

What do you know about each person on your team that might help you during times of change?

_____

_____

How would you describe your team culture now? How do you want it to be? (Team culture is how a team works toward a common goal and how they treat each other.)

_____

_____

What do you need to do to build the team culture you want and get to know your team members?

_____

_____

How soon will you do those things?

_____

_____

Capture additional thoughts and big ideas in the journal section in the back of this book.

Other related words: Acknowledgment, Culture, Emotions, Environment, Expectations, Habit, Mindset, Resistance

COACH

*Someone who creates a collaborative partnership
that holds the person's goals/dreams up high and
supports that person in achieving them*

—Cheryl Smith, executive coach and
cofounder of Leadscape Learning

When we decided that we wanted to write a book about coaching, we had in mind a very specific kind of coach—a leader-coach. There are all kinds of coaches; our expertise is in the area of leadership coaching. We are often asked to define what it means to be a coach, so when we answer that question, our definition is based on leaders who coach. Though each of us would define leadership coaching a little bit differently, we all agree that there is one person who embodies the word *coach*. She is Cheryl Smith. Cheryl has been our trainer, our guide, our mentor, our coach! She is our aspiration and inspiration. Much of what is written in this chapter comes from observing, learning from, being mentored and coached by Cheryl. We would like to dedicate this chapter to you, Cheryl. Thank you for your encouragement and for being the role model of a great leader-coach!

Maybe a good place to begin is to tell you what we are *not* writing about. We are *not* writing about the following:

Sports Coach

When we first started teaching the skills of coaching to our company leaders, there was a great deal of resistance by our leaders to attend the training. Leaders immediately would bring up a famous sports coach and would say things like "I already coach my folks. I coach every day. I had a coach when I played _____ (name the sport). I coach my child's team."

It was quite frustrating to try to explain that a sports coach is not the same as a leader-coach. A sports coach is an expert in his sport. He holds the game plan; he assigns positions. The agenda sits with the sports coach. A sports coach *tells* people what to do more often than asking for input.

Mentor

A mentor is someone who shares their knowledge and can use their influence to support those that they mentor. The mentor is someone who is considered by others as the go-to person for insight and wisdom about a particular topic or position. A few paragraphs down, we will distinguish in greater detail the difference between a mentor and leader-coach.

Consultant

Consultants are those who are considered to have a high level of expertise in a certain area that others find valuable. They are hired to give their advice and input in their area of expertise.

Counselor/Therapist

Counselors/therapists are professionally trained to work with people to promote better mental and emotional health. They use their training to help guide people to a desired mental or emotional outcome.

We are writing about this:

Leader-Coach

This is someone who creates a collaborative partnership and sets clear goals and desired outcomes. A great leader-coach helps create positive energy and momentum. They know when to come alongside to encourage and celebrate. They also know when to step in to direct or hold someone accountable. A leader-coach is not necessarily the subject-matter expert. In fact, they may not know much about your topic or profession. They do not necessarily believe they have all the answers, but rather, they believe the person being coached holds the answer most often. A leader-coach will *ask* more than they tell. They are engaged listeners and willing to hear different perspectives and insights. They can be trusted with others' confidences and struggles. They will be your advocate and truth-teller.

Though we shared our thoughts of what a leader-coach is not, we are not implying that a leader-coach cannot be a sports coach, mentor, consultant, or counselor/therapist. Does that sound contradictory? Being a leader-coach is choosing to show up in any circumstance to ask thought-provoking questions, listen, believe the other person has insight and solutions, and to partner with them to reach the best plan or answer. You may be an expert in your profession, but you can choose to be a leader-coach by choosing to put that expertise and your knowledge to the side so you can engage another person to help them grow, be a better problem solver, or get their perspective. Whether you are a sports coach, mentor, consultant, counselor/therapist, or a new-to-the-role or experienced leader in an organization, you can choose to be a leader-coach—and we hope that you do. We promise that this book can give you the tools to make it happen.

Tips

Get some training. Coaching requires skills and techniques. There are numerous coaching organizations that can help you. You can contact the International Coaching Federation (ICF) for a list of organizations. You can also contact one of us—Coaches3. Our contact information is in our "Last Word" chapter.

Ask. Ask a question instead of giving direction or input. A simple question like "What are your thoughts about this?" can create a productive dialogue.

Be curious. The way to be curious is to ask questions.

Focus on listening. Listen more than you talk.

Resist giving the answer. Don't always be the answer guy or gal. Empower others to problem solve by asking for their input.

Invest. Remember coaching someone is an investment that will have great ROI.

Get a Coach. That will be the best investment that you will ever make.

Example

I had been assigned to a leader who was very resistant to being coached and had no interest in becoming a leader-coach. He was aware that the organization was trying to create a leader-coach culture, and he was definitely not on board. He was known for his organizational expertise and was a great mentor. Our first visits were unproductive. He wasn't rude or hard to have a conversation with, but he let me know that he "saw right through" all the questions that I asked. I stayed the course, showing up every two weeks, asking some of the same questions. This particular day, I asked him this question: "What's keeping you up at night?"

He paused for a bit as I waited in silence. He said, "I think the company is trying to get rid of some of us. Is that true?"

It opened the door for our first real coaching session. My response was not a statement, but a question, which led to more questions and a deeper understanding of this person that I was coaching. Over the next few months, the trust and our relationship grew. He became an advocate for coaching and attended the company's training program. He required all his leaders to attend. He would often tell leaders who reported to him that his biggest time of growth was when he realized the value of having a coach and the importance of coaching others. He stated he saw more growth in people when he showed up as a coach than when he was only mentoring or sharing his expertise. He would often say, "I still want to be the smartest man in the room. but I've learned that the best way to do that is to ask more questions and then listen."

—Coach JoAnn

When leaders attended our company coaching training, they often referred to coaching as something that they did. They said, "I am going to put my coaching hat on." *Doing* coaching versus *being* a coach is much different. Doing coaching is technique/skill driven. You follow a model and insert it when you think that it is appropriate or beneficial. And these are necessary skills to coach. However, you, the leader, are still driving the agenda. Being a coach is how you show up—fully present, collaborative, and building rapport. A leader-coach does not hold tightly to his or her own agenda. It is important to note here that there will be times a leader does have an agenda that must be stated and followed. If that is the case, be clear about that agenda. When you are a coach, you seek a two-way partnership with the person you are coaching. You are willing to go deeper—dig underneath the surface information. Getting leaders to make that shift from *doing* to *being* was tough for some of them. They pushed back and said that the kind of coaching that we were asking them to subscribe to was like handing over their authority. They reminded us that they were hired for their positions because they knew how to get things done and for their knowledge and expertise. Master Coach Cheryl Smith once told a group of us who were trying to create a culture of coaching that "power and position can be very seductive. Being a coach can sound like 'abdicating your throne.'" We believe we saw that play out for many leaders. It was a paradigm shift that some were unwilling to make.

Studies show that an organization that has a coaching culture tends to be more creative, innovative, and productive. Employees whose leader shows up as a coach are more engaged and empowered. These employees will give more of their discretionary energy and will stay with an organization. Want to try being a leader-coach? It all starts with you.

Reflection Questions

Are you ready to *be* a leader-coach? What is getting in your way?

———————————————————————————————

———————————————————————————————

Do you have a coach? If not, why?

———————————————————————————————

———————————————————————————————

Would the people who report to you call you a leader-coach? What attributes would they assign to you?

_____

_____

What kind of coaching training have you attended? What additional training do you need?

_____

_____

Capture additional thoughts and big ideas in the journal section in the back of this book.

Other related words: Culture, Environment, Habit (actually, we recommend studying all of them)

CULTURE

The set of shared attitudes, values, goals, and practices that characterizes an institution or organization

—Merriam-Webster.com

While scrolling through LinkedIn, a quote attributed to management consultant and writer Peter Drucker popped up. It said, "Culture eats strategy for breakfast, operational excellence for lunch, and everything else for dinner." That will stop you in your tracks. We don't believe that this quote means that strategy is not important. It is reminding leaders that the culture you create is just as important.

We have seen teams and businesses that instill a coaching culture thrive. This type of culture is linked to higher engagement and better financial performance. Coaching is ranked high as a valuable skill for leaders. What does a coaching culture look like? The teams we have worked with show a desire to learn, willingness to improve, ability to grow from mistakes, straightforward, two-way dialogue, and trust. There is an expectation that constructive feedback will be provided, questions will be asked, and discovery will occur. When a coaching culture is in place, people feel included, and results are achieved.

Why create a coaching culture? Leaders who have done it tell us the following:

- Coaching conversations offer built-in accountability. We talk about expectations, desired outcomes, actions, what might get in the way, and when things need to be done. We offer our support and talk about check-ins, if appropriate. It's a much easier accountability discussion later if they don't follow through on their commitment.

- People are actively engaged and empowered. There is a feeling of commitment and not just compliance.

- Innovation occurs. Let's get real: the people who are closer to the work have great ideas. Why not tap into their creative thoughts and opinions?

- Frankly, there is more productivity. One leader shared that they started to notice that when they were out of the office the work kept getting done. People weren't waiting for them to get back to take next steps or figure out what to do if they hit a barrier. The employees started coaching themselves and each other.

Transitioning to a coaching culture can take time. Some leaders perceive coaching as giving up control, which makes them uncomfortable. It can be harder to ask questions than just tell people what to do, and leaders are often afraid they will not be seen as an expert. These perceived barriers can hinder them in building a coaching culture. Remember what kind of leader you want to be and what is going to get you there. On the Craig Groeschel Leadership Podcast, he said something that perked up our ears: "Your culture is a combination of what you create and what you allow. It's up to you."

Tips

Assume positive intent. Give people the benefit of the doubt. Assume that they have positive intentions, discover the details, and clarify the bigger picture. You may discover that the other person was indeed committed and competent. Let's face it: we can be the first to jump to blame or righteous indignation. That's not going to get us what we need.

Be a leader-coach. Remember that a culture does not happen overnight. It starts with you. Model the behaviors you expect consistently. Take a coach approach in your conversations and meetings, work on building trust, acknowledge people for progress and work well done, and step up to tough conversations. Find others who are committed to creating a coaching culture and work together to get it done.

Slow down. Until you create new habits, you may need to slow down and make sure you are approaching situations like a coach. Are you asking questions instead of solving the problem? Are you acknowledging? Are you listening? If you are more intentional about doing things, soon you won't even have to think about it—it will become second nature.

Coach everyone. We believe strongly that coaching is for everyone. Avoid the mindset that coaching is just for executives or leaders. Every employee can benefit from coaching, and every leader can be a leader-coach for their team. Why wouldn't you want the same level of engagement and productivity from all your employees that coaching enables in higher positions?

Example

I was talking with a new leader I had met through a preleadership program where she was introduced to coaching, and she really took to it. She told me she wanted to create a coaching culture for her new team. I told her that I knew she believed in the power of coaching and wanted to know how she was going to establish her mindset for her new role. She looked at me quizzically and replied, "I'm going to be curious and believe that people hold the answers to their own problems." She then shared that she was going to ask more questions and be a good listener from the start.

I got a call about a month later asking if I could please meet with her again. Things weren't quite going as she had expected. As soon as I asked her what was going on, it all spilled out. "This is much harder than I thought it was going to be. I want to tell them what to do, I want to solve their problems. I'm the leader. I should be the expert. I'm making assumptions. It's obvious I'm judging them. I haven't even gotten to focusing on development opportunities. I'm failing miserably at this."

Of course, she was not failing. She had reverted back to old habits, and honestly, it had only been a month. After I pointed out the timing, she set a plan of action, and we talked about what success would look like at different time frames. She had a plan for shifting her mindset, for staying on track, measuring progress, and some coaching questions to have in her back pocket if she needed them. Even though we were going to meet periodically, she also identified a leader she felt was good at coaching, and she asked them to be her mentor.

This leader is now an executive. She has continued to model coaching and has created a coaching culture with each new assignment she was given. She often tells me that coaching is contagious. Her favorite thing is mentoring new leaders.

—Coach Debby

Reflection Questions

How will you shift to a coaching mindset?

_____

_____

How will you create a coaching culture for your team?

_____

_____

What does success look like and at what time frames?

_____

_____

How will you celebrate your journey to coaching culture wins?

_____

_____

What might hold you back from creating a coaching culture, and how will you overcome those barriers?

_____

_____

What will be your question to ask when you hear, "What do you want me to do?"

_____

Leaders are continuous learners. What will you do to continue your learning?

_____

_____

Capture thoughts and big ideas in the journal section in the back of this book.

Other related words: Accountability, Acknowledgment, Barriers, Environment, Expectations, Integrity, Language, Listen, Trust

CURIOSITY

The desire to learn or know about anything; inquisitiveness

—FREEDICTIONARY.COM

ONE OF THE reasons we use a word like *curiosity* is to help us as leader-coaches stay in positive and productive mental places.

When coaching, you have the power to choose your mind-set when working with your team and people who need coaching. You can approach problem solving with your team in a way that is judgmental or accusatory, or you can approach problem solving with curiosity and a desire to get to the cause of the concern.

There are times in the workplace when emotions are part of the equation. We should be aware of our emotions and the emotions of others. We should learn to manage ourselves to a place of curiosity instead of getting angry, frustrated, mad, or impatient.

When we use a word like *curiosity*, some people may think we are prying into the personal lives of our employees. Nothing could be further from the truth. As professionals, we should understand the line between being curious and being nosy. When you are being curious, you are asking questions for the benefit of the person. You are trying to help them consider things that they have not thought of or spent much time thinking about before. Being nosy is asking questions that benefit you or cause the person to reveal things that are not related to work or the current matter you are discussing. As the leader, you have the responsibility of knowing what is appropriate and staying on the right side of that line.

We want people to understand that they bring their whole self to work, and we are interested in their overall health and well-being, not just their performance at work. If a person is having personal issues that impact them or their job performance, you may need to coach them on the impacted work behaviors and refer them to the appropriate resources to address their personal concerns. Remain curious and engaged with the employee to identify what the true concern is and support them in getting to the root cause of any issues addressed.

As leader-coaches, we should be curious enough to

- take interest in a person's success;

- hear their side of the story before we jump to our own conclusion;

- hear the rest of the story;

- help the person investigate;

- go down a path of self-discovery; and

- consider that we may not know the answer.

Curiosity indicates a willingness to learn more. Sometimes in coaching, we stop at the surface and never get to the root cause of the concerns. We may be dealing with the symptoms and not the real underlying issues. When a person continues to be stuck in a behavior pattern, being curious, and helping them get to the root cause of what is going on will be the best use of your time and the person's time.

Ask questions from a place of curiosity when a person expresses emotion about a certain subject. When emotions come, we should pause and get curious. We should ask questions and listen while the person examines why the emotions came up. There are times when you are coaching a person and a certain word may trigger a response from the person. When this happens, as their leader-coach, you should be curious. Why did they react to that word? Why did they react to that phrase? It could be words such as *failure, regret, messed up, let us down, disappointed in you,* or *afraid* that trigger a negative response.

Sometimes when we are coaching around performance issues, we may be dealing with problems that have occurred time and time again. We may be starting to feel frustrated with the person. If the person picks up on the frustration, they may not be able to be completely open and honest with you about the situation. Many people are more concerned about not getting in trouble than getting things done. When you start to experience feelings of frustration, shift that into curiosity by asking yourself questions and by asking questions of the person you are coaching

When a person is curious, they want to know more. They want to understand. They want to get beyond the surface and see how thing really work. In coaching, our curiosity helps us get beyond the surface issues and identify what is at the heart of the matter. We help the person get beyond managing the symptoms to working on the underlying cause.

Tips

Be Prepared. Before you have a coaching conversation, spend some time in a state of curiosity, thinking through your approach, and preparing for the conversation

Be Respectful. While you are coaching and asking questions, you can be curious and respectful of the person you are coaching. If you ask a question that the other person perceives as personal or not relevant, you should respect the person and take a different line of questioning. Ultimately, you are not trying to solve the employee's personal problems, but you are trying to identify causes for workplace behaviors you have been observing.

Check your intentions. As a leader who is using a coaching approach, having a healthy amount of curiosity about the person and the topic you are discussing demonstrates a certain level of interest. People want to know that you care about them and your curiosity is based on a desire to see the person move forward in their performance and career.

Manage your emotions. When you are taking a coaching approach and asking questions from a place of curiosity versus a place of anger or frustration, this will help you as the leader-coach to manage and keep your emotions in check and be in a better place of self-management. When you start feeling emotional inside about the coaching situation or the person being coached, don't allow your emotions to hijack the conversation. This is a time where you need to take a step back and assess why you are feeling emotional, and it could be a time for you to seek coaching for yourself.

Stay Engaged. Approaching the conversation with curiosity helps you stay engaged. If you are genuinely interested in helping the person discover what the root cause of the issue is, asking questions based on curiosity will help you stay engaged and on track in the coaching conversation.

To stay in a place of curiosity, ask yourself these questions.

- Question for self:
  - What are my intentions for this conversation?
  - Why am I feeling this emotion? Is my emotion going to benefit this situation?
  - How can I be sure what I say encourages the person versus discourages them?

- Ask the other person these questions:
  - What do you think could be causing this?
  - What have you tried before?
  - What are you willing to do to overcome this?
  - What could be causing you to feel...?
  - You seemed to have a reaction to this word or phrase. Can you tell me more about that?

Example

I was working with someone who was considered a person with high potential for leadership opportunities. When I was coaching this person, they came to a point where they were not pursuing career opportunities. They would say they wanted to advance in their career, but they were not taking action. During one of our conversations, I asked permission to pause our conversation and talk about why they were not moving forward. Of course, they said they didn't know. So I thought I would ask a curious question. I asked them, "What is under that rock?"

They said, "What do you mean?"

I said, "What is under that rock? What is the thing you are afraid to see if you lift it up and examine what is under there? What do you think is the thing under that rock that you really don't want to deal with?"

That question opened up a very productive space in our coaching relationship. The person acknowledged that they felt a lot of external pressure to excel and extending themselves to a point of potential failure caused them to be fearful of taking risks in their career. From that point forward, we were able to talk about what was really going on, and no longer in the cycle of missed opportunities.

—*Coach Kevin*

Reflection Questions

What are the three things you can do to improve how you use curiosity when coaching?

_____

_____

When you ask the question *why*, does it come from a place of curiosity or judgment? How can you ask the question and maintain your curiosity?

_____

_____

What questions would you ask if you were being curious?

_____

_____

What is the impact on others when they seeing you using curiosity while coaching?

_____

_____

Capture additional thoughts and big ideas in the journal section in the back of the book.

Other related words: Accountability, Discovery, Listen, Questions

DISCOVERY

The process of finding information, a place,
or an object, especially for the first time

—THE CAMBRIDGE DICTIONARY

IN COACHING, YOU are supporting people through a process in which they can discover new paths forward. It could be as simple as helping someone figure out the most efficient way to accomplish a task or supporting someone who is developing the skills they need for a new career opportunity. Many times, people are stuck or having limited success because their current way of thinking or doing is not producing the outcomes they desire.

The person may not know of another way to do it. With coaching, you could simply ask them questions such as these:

- What are some other things you have considered to solve the problem?

- Have you faced a similar challenge in the past? What did you do to overcome that challenge?

- What would happen if you fully commit to the plan you have developed?

- What would you do if you could not fail?

As coaches, we believe most people have ideas about what they would like to do or who they would like to become. There may be things holding them back. Some people need help in discovering the possibilities:

- People may have doubts or lack confidence

- Others lack disciplined effort or desire

- Some may be in a place of fear, based on prior bad experiences

- The person may lack knowledge or skill

- Some people may lack resources (technology, social capital, proper equipment)

When it comes to performance in the workplace, we believe most people come to work and want to do a good job. We don't think that anyone wants to be an underperformer at work. We also believe some people lack the knowledge, skills, and disciplined effort to achieve success in the workplace. These employees/leaders need someone to spend time with them, examining their current thinking or the approach they are taking to their work. As a leader-coach, there will be times when you help a person discover by listening to them and asking them questions to develop their thoughts. Sometimes while they are responding to your question, they will self-discover what works for them. When this happens, it is evidence that the person is engaged in resolving the concern for themselves and demonstrates personal growth. You have heard the phrase "you could see the lights come on" when a person gains insight or has a discovery. You can see it in their expression. When this happens, a person can truly own the discovery of their path because they came up with it themselves.

Coaching can be thought of as a verbal, problem-solving

methodology where the leader-coach supports a person on their path of learning how to think critically and find answers to their problems.

When we thought about the word *discover* as it relates to coaching, we thought about becoming aware of something that already exists. A discovery is something new to the person who finds it.

When you are coaching a person and asking them one question at a time, with each question you ask you are helping them through a process of self-discovery. There is something there that the person does not see.

When you coach people, you ask them questions to help them discover *their* answer or their path, not yours. In cases where there is one right answer, it may be best to tell the person instead of going through the motions of coaching. Coaching is a great approach, but it is not the answer to every situation. If there are multiple answers or several approaches to solve a problem, use coaching to help the person discover the path that is best for them. Asking questions can be an effective way to build the competence and confidence of the person you are working with.

> **Tips**
>
> **Use Open-ended Questions.** Asking open-ended questions is one of the most effective ways to get people to self-discover. Asking yes-or-no questions may lead people down dead-end paths. Open-ended questions allow or require a person to think about their response and the words they need to answer the question.
>
> Examples of open-ended questions:
>
> Closed: Did you follow the manual?
>
> Open: What resources did you use to resolve the problem?
>
> Closed: Do you want to have a future here?
>
> Open: What type of work would you like to do in the future?
>
> **Encourage Thinking.** Encourage people to think during the

coaching conversation. Here are some examples of how you can do that:

- Before we get started today, please write down the three things you want most from this conversation.

- Take a few minutes and imagine what it would be like if everything were going right at work. What would that look like?

- What would it take for you to be successful at this task?

- What concerns you most about this responsibility?

Ask Unique Questions. Don't be afraid to ask off-the-wall or lateral-thinking questions such as the following:

- What would you do if failure was not an option?

- What would Wonder Woman or Superman do to solve this problem?

- If you could do anything you wanted to do to resolve this, what would you do?

Don't Be a Problem Solver. When you start a coaching session, leave your preconceived notions about what is best for the person out of the conversation. Only contribute your ideas and opinions with them when the person has exhausted theirs, if they are still stuck, and are open to receiving your input.

Invest Time in Brainstorming. Coach them through a brainstorming exercise:

- Have the person come to the meeting with ideas on how to solve the problem.

- During the conversation have the person spend two minutes writing down as many solutions or ideas related to their problem as they can.

Ask Exploration and Discovery Questions. Consider asking the person being coached some of these questions:

- Which task should be done first and why?

- Which task could be done last and why?

- What would it take to get both done in a timely manner?

- Which of these tasks has the most value at this time?

- Who could help with this task?

- What would have to change to get both of these done?

- What other ways can you make this work?

- What is the impact if one of these tasks doesn't get done before the other assignment?

- What could help you with this task?

- What are the areas you need to develop more knowledge or skill to get these tasks done?

Give me an example:

I was coaching someone who did not want to take any risks with their career, yet they were not satisfied with their current role. Since I knew the person was not satisfied with their current job. I started coaching them on career exploration. The person was working on being more confident and taking risks. During one of our coaching conversations, I asked the person where confidence comes from. The person said, "Through experience."

We brainstormed on ways the person could get experience that would boost their confidence.

Through our coaching conversation, the person decided they would interview with another company. Interviewing with another company created a low-risk scenario for the person to practice their interviewing skills and to explore the external job market. This opportunity gave them other people's perspectives on their talents and real-world experiences interviewing.

The person interviewed and made it through a couple of rounds of interviews. They ultimately did not take the job, and I am thankful for that. I wanted them to stay with us but knew this person needed to do something to jump-start their career. In the process, the person discovered that they had a lot to offer to other companies and to our company. They had to take a hard look at their skills and their potential.

A short while later, the person made an unexpected and significant career move within the company. I am sure that the practice and confidence the person gained from their external interviewing experience helped them prepare for our internal process. Through this coaching process, the person discovered there are many ways to gain experience. They also discovered what they wanted from a career and that they had the talent to be competitive externally and internally.

—Coach Kevin

Many times, people need coaching when they have not stopped to take the time to think through their problem. They are just working harder and not smarter. When someone asks you a question, instead of just giving them the answer, pause and ask them a few thoughtful coaching questions. Sometimes, we use questions that are restrictive or create constraints to bring out efficiencies. Other times, we ask questions to create more expansive thinking to broaden possibilities. You can lead with a question such as one of the following:

- If you had one less day to approach this, what could you do?
- If your budget was unlimited, how would you solve the customer's concern?

Get their thoughts before you give them yours. Take them through the process of self-discovery, and more often than not, the person will find the solutions that will work best for them. When a person uncovers their own solution, it improves their critical-thinking skills. The person learns how to find their own answers to help them in their tasks for today and set them up to be able to use similar thinking skills for problems of the future.

Reflection Questions

How can you support people through the process of discovery?

What are the open-ended questions you want to ask?

How do you allow space for people to explore creative solutions?

After you ask coaching questions, are you allowing enough time and silence for discovery? What tells you that?

What do you need to do to manage yourself when you become aware that you are trying to control the process and the outcomes?

_____

_____

Capture additional thoughts and big ideas in the journal section in the back of the book.

Other related words: Accountability, Acknowledgment, Barriers, Environment, Expectations, Integrity, Language, Listen, Trust

EMOTIONS & EMOTIONAL INTELLIGENCE

Emotional intelligence refers to the ability to identify and manage one's own emotions, as well as the emotions of others.

—*Psychology Today*[3]

PEOPLE HAVE A broad range of emotions; from happy to sad and excited to fearful. We all have various ways of dealing with our emotions and different manners of expressing our emotions. Since understanding our emotions is key to success, we should be intelligent about our emotions. Emotional intelligence has many definitions. The authors of *Emotional Intelligence 2.0* define emotional intelligence, or EQ, as your ability to identify and understand emotions in yourself and others, and to use this awareness to manage your responses and relationships.[4]

Being intelligent about emotions is a life and business skill. Your ability to manage your emotions can determine how you relate to the world, and it can impact how others relate to you. In a coaching

---

3   https://www.psychologytoday.com/us/basics/emotional-intelligence.

4   Bradberry, Travis, and Jean Greaves. *Emotional Intelligence 2.0*. San Diego: TalentSmart, 2009.

conversation, there are times when you are talking about sensitive things, such as job performance, personal barriers, compensation, and career potential. Some of these conversations may become emotionally charged. We need to be able to recognize when we are having an emotional response and when employees are becoming emotional during a coaching conversation. Employees will often bring emotions into the workplace. As a leader-coach, you need to be able to identify the differences and coach the person on areas that impact work and refer them to resources for support for issues and concerns that are impacting them in their personal life

Being intelligent about emotions helps us adapt our behavior during coaching conversations. When you are coaching and things start to get emotional, the last thing you want to do is *ignore* the emotions. If you ignore emotions, you may appear indifferent or callous. Acknowledging emotions helps the other person understand that you are engaged and you are aware of how they are being impacted by what is happening. When you acknowledge your emotions and the emotions of the person, you increase your ability to be able to manage the emotions. You must first manage your own emotions before you can help someone manage theirs.

If you are not able to manage your own emotions, you are in a danger zone. You could cause harm to your career, your relationships, and your ability to lead effectively. If you ignore the emotions of others, you may push people away or be seen as someone who is out of touch, even mean or uncaring. If your employees develop these opinions about you, it will be hard to lead and influence them. If we allow our emotions to become out of control, we will do and say things that may harm our ability to influence our employees. Think of a boss who has frequent, big, emotional blow-ups while the organization is touting an open-door policy and leaders being approachable. When this happens, it is hard for employees to trust that they can go to their leaders with problems or concerns.

As an emotionally intelligent leader, you must know what to look for in yourself and others when feeling and expressing your emotions. Also, when you are coaching, be aware when you sense a change in the emotional state of the conversation. Do you notice a physical, behavioral, or emotional change in yourself? Do you notice those changes in others? When you notice changes, you should slow down and ask yourself why. *What has caused these changes? Why am I experiencing these changes?* Once you increase your ability to be aware of emotional shifts, you will be able to change and align your behavior to match the outcomes you want for the coaching conversation. This results in the successful achievement of the outcomes you want for yourself, the employee, and the organization.

As the leader, you are the person responsible for managing the coaching conversation. Be aware of the situation and the conditions that exist. You are responsible for managing your emotions first and the emotional climate of the discussion second. To increase your competence as a coach, you have to be aware of your own emotions and be willing to move into self-management. You should also be alert and watch for shifts in the emotions of the other person, know when to pause, and take time to examine the environment. Consider using the coaching approaches we are discussing in this book and specifically think through some of the coaching strategies listed below to get and keep the coaching session on track.

Some of the Strategies We Recommend
Acknowledging the Emotions

It is acceptable to acknowledge emotions during coaching. When you feel yourself getting emotional, you can simply pause, take a short break, and get yourself together mentally and emotionally. There is truth in the old adage of counting to ten before you react. Asking questions forces you and the person you are coaching to make a mental shift from the emotional portions of the brain to the logical, executive functioning parts of the brain. If you notice the employee having an emotional response, you can say, "You seem to be having a response to something that was said. Do we need to take a break and resume later, or would you like to talk about how you are feeling?" Acknowledging the emotions will be more effective than ignoring them. When emotions show up, they become part of the conversation whether we like it or not and whether we pretend we don't notice them or don't want to deal with them. Learning how to skillfully manage your emotions and respecting the emotions of the other person will help you build strong interpersonal relationships and give you an advantage in leading productive coaching conversations. You will find a list of resources that will help you in increasing your ability to manage your emotions in the Resources section of this book.

Reconciling the Emotions

If you notice the employee having an emotional reaction during a coaching session, you should inquire about their emotions. If they indicate it was something you said or did that caused the reaction, you should spend time to understand why. Once you get an understanding, if you actually did do something wrong, you should acknowledge your behavior and apologize. You may need to clarify your intent or message. The emotion could be caused by a simple misunderstanding that happened. Pausing and clearing up a misunderstanding will keep the employee engaged and allow you to continue in a productive way. Only return to the conversation after the emotional situation has been reconciled. If the emotional response persists, you could consider ending and rescheduling.

Coaching often involves discussions about things that are very important to you and the person being coached. There are times when employees will perceive some of these conversations as getting in trouble, or they may feel their job may be at risk if they express their ideas and/or emotions honestly. Since the stakes may be high at times, being emotionally intelligent is one of the foundational skills of coaching. Being aware of your emotions and having the ability to adapt your behavior will impact the quality and effectiveness of your coaching. Acknowledging and being empathetic toward the emotions of others will help you establish positive workplace relationships and increase your ability to influence and coach others.

Tips

As you read through these tips, understand that they apply equally to you and to the person you are coaching.

Stay alert for cues or changes. Look for cues or changes in any of these:

- emotions (look out for fear, frustration, and anger)
- physical (body language and posture, change in facial expression)
- behaviors (raising or lowering voice, finger pointing, loss of eye contact)

When you notice shifts in emotions, identify the emotion:

- What emotion am I feeling?
- Is there something we need to talk about? What emotions are you feeling?

Determining the cause of the emotion. Ask questions to determine the cause of the emotion:

- Why am I feeling this emotion during this conversation?
- Can we talk about where that emotion is coming from?
- What is causing you to feel this emotion during this conversation?

Managing the response. Pause before you react.

- What should I do to manage my emotions and move the conversation in a productive direction?

- What do we need to do right now to move this conversation forward in a positive manner?

- Can we continue this conversation or do we need to take a break for a moment?

Develop your knowledge and self-awareness.

In our coaching experience, we encourage people to read books and articles about emotional intelligence. We also encourage people to take an emotional-intelligence assessment. These assessments give you an awareness of where you are with your emotional intelligence.

Assessments give you insights into your thinking and behaviors. Along with insights on your behaviors, most assessments provide ideas on behaviors you can practice to develop your self-awareness and increase your ability to self-manage your emotions. There will be some things you are good at when it comes to emotional intelligence and you should leverage those strengths in coaching conversations. Then there will be some areas for improvement, and we encourage you to talk with someone you trust within the organization or outside of the organization (yes, talk with some who will coach you). Tell them what you are working on related to emotional intelligence, develop a plan, and schedule some time for accountability checks.

- Read books on emotional intelligence
  - *Emotional Intelligence: Why It Can Matter More Than IQ,* Daniel Goleman
  - *Primal Leadership: Unleashing the Power of Emotional Intelligence,* Daniel Goleman
  - *Emotional Intelligence 2.0,* Travis Bradberry and Jean Greaves

- Take an emotional-intelligence assessment
  - *Emotional Intelligence 2.0*, Travis Bradberry and Jean Greaves
  - EQ in Action Profile Assessment—Learning in Action

Example

I was leading a highly productive team of assistants. One of the most productive members of my team, Claire, was having some problems getting along with others. Claire's approach to work was hard driving and she had high expectations of herself and others. We got to a point where her approach was causing stress for her teammates… and for me.

I scheduled a meeting with Claire to talk about team dynamics and our working relationship. I was not looking forward to this meeting because Claire could be confrontational. I went in mentally prepared for a battle. When the meeting started, I told her my concerns and she defensively held her position. I began asking coaching questions about her situation like "Where did your work ethic and high expectations come from?" and "What does having a job and working really mean to you?" As she answered, I could see and hear her body language and tone change. Some tears were even shed. As we continued the conversation, I clarified my expectations of her and told her about our company's employee assistance plan resources.

We had a real breakthrough in our working relationship and Claire agreed to shift how she related to the team and to me. Sometimes emotions catch you completely off guard. That day I was prepared for everything except, the emotions

—Coach Kevin

Reflection Questions

How can you improve your emotional intelligence?

_____

_____

What are your blind spots when it comes to emotional intelligence?

_____

_____

What are your emotional triggers?

_____

_____

What can you do to better manage your emotions?

_____

_____

Who can give you good feedback on your emotional intelligence?

_____

_____

What emotions do you express in the workplace?

_____

_____

How is your team being impacted by your emotions?

_____

_____

Capture additional thoughts and big ideas in the journal section in the back of the book.

Other related words: Curiosity, Listen, Goals, Mindset

ENVIRONMENT

---

*The surroundings or conditions in which
a person lives, works or operates*

—CAMBRIDGE DICTIONARY

THE WORK ENVIRONMENT of an organization gets more press in today's world than it did in previous generations. There are reasons for that:

- numerous studies on the health and welfare of employees

- competition for good employees

- employees being more vocal about their personal values and goals

- the organization's reputation among its employees being broadcast through various media platforms

In previous generations, potential employees didn't inquire about the work environment. That is not the case in today's world. There are now companies that exist solely to inform the public about the environment and culture of any given organization. They regularly produce studies of the impact that a work environment has on employee's engagement and the productivity of an organization.

The Gallup Organization is one of those organizations that has done major studies on employee engagement. One of their important findings was the impact and importance of the environment of the organization as a whole and the environment created by individual leaders for their teams. For employees to be actively engaged, the environment has to be responsive to the needs and perceptions of the employees. Gallup also found that when leaders *coached* their teams, the employee-engagement index rose. And, we know that the more someone is engaged in their work, the more productive they are and the more likely they are to stay with that organization.

There are plenty of studies that show that coaching can have a positive impact on employee engagement and the organization's bottom line. The studies also state that if there is not a conducive and supportive environment in the organization that encourages coaching, coaching will not thrive and flourish. Therefore, there are two questions that should be addressed:

- How do you define a successful coaching environment?
- How do you create it?

It's hard to define a successful coaching environment but easy to feel when you've achieved it. Imagine you are going to a restaurant to have dinner with someone significant in your life. You enter the restaurant, and the first thing you notice is a sense of calm, yet there is focused activity. The tables have crisp, white linens with simple, elegant settings. The background music is soothing and easy to hear. You're escorted to your table by the host who welcomes you, inquires about your well-being—not too chatty but open and friendly. You're seated at your table, and you're approached by your server who is deliberate and warm. She has just the right balance of showing up at your table at the right time when you need something and knowing when to let you linger undisturbed. Your evening was perfect. The restaurant environment helped facilitate a wonderful, romantic evening with someone important to you. You chose this restaurant because you had a specific, desired outcome and the restaurant environment was very important to that outcome. This would not have been the same experience at a fast-food place or a nightclub. This simple example demonstrates that you must have the right environment for certain outcomes. So it is with coaching. You must have the right environment for it to flourish.

Here are some thoughts about what a successful coaching environment looks like:

- The organization and individual leaders believe in and support collaboration at all levels.

- People at all levels consistently seek and willingly give feedback.

- Professional and personal growth is modeled and encouraged.

- Coaching is seen by leaders as part of their responsibility.

- There is a high level of trust among all levels of the organization.

- Leaders view themselves as coaches. They don't *do* coaching; they *are* coaches.

A successful coaching environment doesn't emerge because there is an edict from senior leadership. It definitely does not happen overnight. Organizations and individual leaders must be consistent and deliberate in creating an environment that encourages and supports coaching.

Tips

The following tips are for the organization and/or individual leaders:

Provide/seek training. Give all leaders the basic skills of coaching.

Support employees. Equip them with skills to be coached effectively.

Seek opportunities. Look for ways leaders can experience good coaching practices (one of the best ways to do this is to give them a coach).

Don't talk about coaching. Do it.

Build on these. Encourage transparency and collaboration; it builds trust.

Reward. Reward small coaching wins and celebrate big wins.

Set the expectation. Set the expectation that leader-coaches are the norm in your organization.

Example

As organizational coaches, we would be assigned a new-to-the-role leader. This could mean someone for whom this is their first opportunity as a formal leader, or it could mean someone who had been promoted from one leadership position into another area of responsibility. Our role as coaches was to support this new leader in acclimating to their new team and responsibilities. We also hoped to assimilate them into the coaching environment. Our goal for this newly assigned leader was for them to become a coach, not just learn and experience the skills of coaching but be a coach. One particular leader who had been a first-line leader for a few years had been promoted to a level up. He decided that he would buy into this "being-a-coach stuff," as he referred to it.

After he went through the coaching workshop to learn the skills, he had an assigned coach. It seemed he was really trying to use the skills that he'd learned in the coaching workshop, and he always showed up for his coaching sessions with his assigned coach. He would talk about how unresponsive his team was to his efforts of coaching. After a couple of months of trying to coach his team, he told his assigned coach that he was ready to give up on trying to coach. We asked if his team could be interviewed to see how the team thought he was doing. The leader agreed.

It was found out rather quickly that his new team had some trust issues with the leader—his reputation had preceded him. He was known by his former team as a micromanager and was very direct in his leadership style. His former team confirmed that there was not a lot of trust. The leader had embraced coaching, but his new team didn't know that. Bottom line—the leader had not created an environment that supported his coaching efforts. Over the next few months, the leader with his coach's support, worked on creating an environment of transparency, trust, and collaboration. His team attended a workshop on how to engage with a leader-coach. Eventually, the team and the leader began to gel and were very productive. The next year, the leader's employee-opinion-survey results reported a significant increase in employee engagement. The leader credited his team and the coaching environment that they had created together.

—Coach JoAnn

If you are trying to create a better coaching environment, here are some questions/suggestions for you to consider:

- If someone walked into your current work environment what sense would they have? What words would they use to describe what they feel or see?

- Pay attention to how your work area changes/shifts when you show up. Do they smile? Do they welcome you into the conversation? What are their reactions to you?

- Do you encourage dialogue and collaboration? Do you ask open-ended questions?

- How would you describe the overall leadership environment that you are part of? Is it open? Collaborative? Welcoming? What do you like about the environment? What would you change?

- What is one thing that you could do to make your environment more conducive to coaching?

Remember the dining experience example? An environment that is welcoming, open, collaborative, intentional, and inclusive will help facilitate the growth of coaches and a coaching environment that will flourish.

Reflection Questions

Is the environment in your organization conducive to coaching? What tells you that?

_____

_____

How are you specifically contributing in creating/sustaining a positive coaching environment?

_____

_____

What could you do to influence a stronger coaching environment among your peers and overall leadership?

_____

_____

Would your team say that the environment is a safe place to ask questions or to innovate and to fail? Ask your team how the environment could be improved. Pick one suggestion and work on it. Then pick another. Check in with your team often to measure the progress.

_____

_____

Capture thoughts and big ideas in the journal section in the back of this book.

Other related words: Culture, Habit, Accountability

EXPECTATIONS

To anticipate or look forward to the coming or occurrence of

—Merriam-Webster.com

Establishing clear expectations is fundamental to every relationship. It does not matter if it is a professional or personal relationship, an informal or formal interaction, we all have expectations of each other whether they be spoken or unspoken. Discussing and setting clear expectations and abiding by those expectations keep us intellectually and emotionally safe and avoids misunderstandings and disappointments.

As a leader who is using coaching to motivate and manage employees, one of your roles is to establish clear expectations. During every performance period, you should have ongoing conversations about expectations with the people who report to you. Employees base most of their workplace behaviors on workplace expectations that have been set by formal or informal leaders in the organizations.

During coaching conversations, leaders establishing clear expectations is critical to the person's success. When coaching, it is good to establish expectations for the conversation. The expectations set are determined by the focus of the conversation. If it is a performance-based conversation, you should set the tone by stating your expectations. If you are discussing development, the person being coached should have an opportunity to help establish the tone for the discussion.

An expectation in coaching is clearly establishing that the employee is ultimately responsible for their workplace behaviors and their performance outcomes. When a person brings a problem to your desk, they should expect that you will give them some coaching (asking good, thought-provoking questions) and maybe some sound advice or guidance and that they will leave your desk or the conversation equipped to solve the problem.

We understand that if they bring a problem to your desk and the resolution of the problem truly lies with you, then you and the person being coached should expect you to own the problem and the solution. Otherwise, the person you are coaching owns their problem and does the work of resolving the issue.

Tips

Use common language with specific examples and agreed-upon timelines. It is important to remember that without clear expectations, it is difficult to hold people accountable for their behavior and their outcomes. We have to communicate our expectations using common language, with specific examples and agreed-upon timelines. We can't expect people to read our minds and know what our unstated expectations are. Some expectations are so basic we may not even consciously remember to share them with people, things such as what time we report to work, which doors to use, how long we take for lunch, even where a person should park their car. However, the initial expectations in the workplace are generally about the job and what needs to be done.

Switching it up. We encourage you to create and communicate

expectations with your team around taking a coaching approach. If you are a person who has used a command-and-control style, when you switch to more of a coaching style, communicate this change to your team. By doing this, you will be establishing your intentions for changing your style. Sharing your intentions to change your behavior will help your employees to know they should expect new behaviors. When your actual behavior does not match your stated desired behavior, your employees can bring these behaviors to your attention and help keep you stay focused on using your new coaching behaviors. You might say, "I know in the past my style has been more direct, and I am going to be working on using more of a coaching-and-collaborative style of communications. You can expect some changes in the way we engage in conversations. I will ask more questions, listen more intently, and work with you on solving the problems that arise in your work."

Clearly and timely communicate changes to expectations. When expectations change, they should be communicated clearly and timely to everyone impacted by the change. No one likes to work on a project just to find out that the goal, target, budget, or timelines have changed and they did not know about it. In a coaching environment, people should expect honesty and respect. Informing people of changing expectations is part of being respectful in the workplace.

Expectations in a leader-coach and employee relationship. When you are in a leader-coach relationship with your employees, there are several areas to consider when establishing expectations. You can use the following topics as a guide to have a conversation with your employees or team about your approach to coaching in the workplace.

Leader-coaches should expect

- honesty;
- commitment from the person being coached;

- thoughtful answers;
- to be silent while the person is thinking;
- mixed reactions when giving feedback;
- people to have struggles and need support; and
- to equip employees with developmental resources.

People being coached should expect

- confidentiality from the leader-coach;
- hard work;
- thought-provoking questions;
- to be required to think outside of the box;
- to be held accountable for commitments;
- respectful and honest feedback;
- clear expectations;
- to have challenges and setbacks; and
- support from leadership.

Example

Coach Kevin shared the following examples of having expectation setting conversations:

If you are opening up a performance-coaching conversation:

Today, we only have about thirty minutes for this conversation. I would like to spend the first half discussing any concerns you have about the project and the second half sharing some of my observations and discussing your path forward. Does that seem like a good use of our time today?

If you are closing a performance-coaching conversation:

I appreciate the good conversation we had today. As we look forward, let's go over our action items. Who is responsible for turning in the final report to Susan? When will this be done? What support do you or the team need from me to meet this deadline? Remember: if the venue changes to the lodge, we will need handouts instead of a PowerPoint presentation; there is no A/V at the lodge.

Be sure to establish who needs to do what and by when. Discuss how you will follow up on the conversation.

Reflection Questions

What do you need to do to establish clear expectations?

_____

_____

What questions could you ask when setting expectations related to performance?

_____

_____

What questions could you ask when setting expectations related to development?

_____

_____

What do people expect from you when they meet or exceed expectations?

_____

_____

What does your team expect from you when they fail to meet expectations? When things go wrong, how can you stay focused on coaching for the future versus looking to blame or punish?

_____

_____

Capture additional thoughts and big ideas in the journal section in the back of the book.

Other related words: Goals, Feedback, Questions, Listen

FEEDBACK

*Information about reactions to a product,
a person's performance of a task, etc., which
is used as a basis for improvement*

—Oxford English Dictionary

Bill Gates, business leader and philanthropist, once said, "We all need people who will give us feedback. That's how we improve."

Leaders must give feedback. This is an area that leaders tell us that they often struggle within their role. There are two ends of the spectrum. The first is that leaders are so harsh with how they give feedback that it is a negative experience that shuts the person down. The other is they are so reluctant to share feedback that the person doesn't understand the feedback they are being given and makes no changes. Neither way will work if you want to get results and build relationships. One of the most important skills you need to learn is how to provide feedback that does not tear down the person you are giving it to and allows them to hear what you are saying.

Some mistakes we see leaders make with giving feedback is that they stop at sharing their observations. In addition to your observations, you should do the following:

- Decide if you need to state your intentions. Does the other person understand why you are providing this feedback?

- Consider your relationship with this person. Is trust in place?

- Include the impact or consequences of how what they did had on things like results, customers, their team, and the organization.

- Stick to the facts and don't include your personal opinions.

Are you missing opportunities to share positive feedback? Too often, leaders only share the things that are not going well. They don't think about letting someone know when they are making a positive impact. They take the no-news-is-good-news approach. If you want people to keep doing the things they are doing that are getting results, tell them and then watch them repeat that behavior and do even better.

At this point, you may be asking what the difference is between feedback and acknowledgment. Both are important skills for leaders to demonstrate. Feedback is more about behaviors you have observed—"I have noticed how you take the time to explain why things need to be done a certain way to your team members. This helps them understand the reason behind the task and they are more motivated to complete it." Acknowledgment is more about who the person is and how they show up. It may touch on their character, attributes, or values. "You are an inspiring leader who makes people feel like they are important."

It's not only about what you have to say. When you are delivering a message or tough feedback, you should enter that conversation equally prepared to listen as much as you talk. You never know what you might learn.

It can be really easy to get in your head and overthink or start telling yourself stories about what you think happened or how you think the other person is going to respond. Not only could you be wrong, but your stories could evoke emotions for you that will not be helpful.

Keep in mind that feedback *is* information. You provide the information and then support the other person in figuring out what to do with it to get the desired results.

Tips

Create an environment where people want and expect feedback. Make sure your intention in providing the feedback is positive. Ask yourself if there is judgment or a personal agenda attached to the feedback. If you have built trust, then when you need to give feedback, the other person will not question why and will feel safe to receive and discuss it. If they feel you have their best interests in mind, they have a better chance of hearing you. If they feel you have an agenda or are trying to manipulate them, all bets are off.

Use a coach approach. Clearly deliver the feedback using neutral, nonjudgmental language so there is little room as possible for misinterpretation of what is being said or for the other person to get defensive. Then ask for their thoughts. It could sound like "What do you think? How could you do better? What is getting in your way? What are you learning?" This will allow you to get a better understanding of how they are doing and how you can support them.

Better yet, ask for their thoughts first. You will find most people will be tougher on themselves than you would have been. Allow them the opportunity to reflect and self-discover. This also makes the pivot to brainstorming solutions feel more natural.

Don't use absolute language. Saying *always* or *never* will allow the other person to dismiss what you are sharing. If they can remember that one time your feedback did not apply, then they will reject what you are saying as incorrect.

Be careful about masking feedback. When we were new supervisors, we were taught the sandwich method for giving feedback. This method suggests that when providing negative feedback, you should tell them something positive, then tell them the negative feedback, and end with something else positive. We believe the intention is to soften the blow of the negative feedback. It's not wrong to share what someone is doing right. They need to hear that. However, if the feedback they really need to hear that will help them gets lost, then this method is not effective. Instead, we recommend that you make sure they understand why you are sharing the feedback (your intention), give the feedback, including the impact of what they did or didn't do had on other people or results, and then ask for their thoughts. We also recommend that you make sure you are providing positive feedback when appropriate and not just constructive feedback. Everyone needs to hear when they are doing well too!

Do some reflection prior to the conversation. What message or feedback do you specifically need to deliver? The more concise and succinct that message or feedback, the better. Consider the outcome you desire. This will help you with your intention.

When was the last time you asked for feedback? Model the behavior you want from others and ask for feedback from your leader, your peers, and your team. It will help you be a better leader and remember what it felt like to be on the receiving end of feedback.

Example

What not to say:

"Look, you are not doing what you need to do. You need to do better. No excuses. We're done here."

This may sound like an extreme example. We've actually heard leaders talk like this. Instead try something like this:

"I want you to be successful in your role. I have noticed that you have not completed three out of the five tasks on our new project. When you miss your deadlines, your team members cannot do their tasks and it puts us behind on completion. I expect that every person completes their tasks on time or lets me know why that might not happen. What is getting in your way of completing your tasks?"

—*Coach Debby*

Reflection Questions

Rate yourself on a scale of 1–5 with 1 being "never" and 5 being "always."

1. I recognize giving feedback as a coaching opportunity.

   _____

2. I am timely in giving feedback.

   _____

3. I avoid giving people feedback.

   _____

4. I am open to listening to people during a feedback session.

   _____

What can you do to move these results more to where you want them?

_____

_____

Work on a real feedback conversation you need to have:
Whom do I need to give feedback to now?

_____

_____

What are the facts of the situation?

_____

_____

What is the behavior they need to have to meet their performance standards?

_____

_____

When will I give them the feedback?

_____

_____

What impact is this having on other things?

_____

_____

What stories am I telling myself?

_____

_____

What outcome do I want from this conversation?

_____

_____

Capture additional thoughts and big ideas in the journal section in the back of this book.

Other related words: Environment, Expectations, Intention, Messaging, Relationships, Trust

FOCUS

To direct one's attention or efforts

—Dictionary.com

THE WORD *FOCUS* has many meanings related to coaching. There are several ways and several instances that require focus. These are a few foundational areas:

- What is my focus as a coach?

- How can I help the person I am coaching stay focused?

- What is the focus of the conversation?

- What is the focus of the coaching engagement?

There are times when staying on task can be difficult. Staying on the same page with the person being coached is important. Ask yourself, *Are we both focused on the same thing?* At times, a person may start to explore another topic or issue rather than the agreed-upon focus that was set at the beginning of the conversation. We have found that checking in with the person during the conversation to ask what they would like to focus on and accomplish during the discussion may be the quickest way to get them back to the agreed-upon topic. An example of that would be that the person is clearly frazzled, or they tell you something is occupying their thoughts. Asking them if they would like to talk through the issue can help clear their mind so they can focus on the agreed-upon topic.

One of the key reasons to stay focused is it helps you get things done and usually get things done faster. We often hear people say coaching takes too much time. One way to manage the time it takes to coach is to be disciplined in staying focused. Here are some helpful suggestions:

- **Focus in the moment.** Some people feel like coaching is this big, huge thing that you must do. Coaching can be as simple as asking the right question at the right time to shift a person's thinking or perspective. Remember: whether it is a scheduled coaching conversation or a coaching opportunity in the flow of work, your focus should be helping that person move forward toward the desired outcomes.

- **Focus on the conversation.** Being in tune with the person you are coaching is essential. Moving in the same direction requires work. You can ask yourself these questions:

  - Are we talking about what we agreed we would be talking about?

  - Is the thing they said they wanted to talk about the real issue?

  - As you are coaching a person, feel free to check in with them to ensure you are still focused on the thing that is most important for them at the time. Their focus may shift and that is okay. Make sure the person is moving in the desired direction and not on a tangent.

- **Focus on the person being coached.** One of the most important things you can do as a leader is to help the person you are coaching stay focused on what they can impact. A friend shared a story about a time when a person came to them complaining about another person. Their response to the complaining person was "How did they respond when you talked with them about this?" This was a powerful way to shift the conversation back to what the person being coached can do in this situation. One of the adages of coaching is you can only coach the person who is in the current coaching conversation. You must coach the person in front of you. You cannot coach the person who is not there.

- **Focus on coaching, not problem solving.** Stay focused on helping the person learn to solve their own problems. Resist the urge to shift back into problem-solving mode. When wrapping up a coaching conversation, focus on setting the stage for future accountability. Remember to establish *who* is responsible for doing *what* by *when*.

- **Focus on behavior.** When coaching, help people focus on the behaviors and habits they need to use to accomplish their goals. Help people establish a clear understanding of what the desired behavior is, the frequency that they should practice that behavior, and when they should practice that behavior.

- **Focus on emotions.** Remember when we talked about emotions and being emotionally intelligent? Sometimes, leaders shy away from emotions and emotional conversations. When you are coaching people and they get emotional about a topic, it may be a clue to explore that topic deeper. Contrary to what we may believe, we need to focus on emotions. For most of us, the things that are important to us are wrapped up in emotions. Along with emotions, there are other things you need to focus on during the conversation: body language, rate of speech, word choice, things that are not being said (or avoided), and facial expressions.

Tips

Be aware of things that keep you from being focused. This could be any of these:

- your biases related to your ideas, attitudes, methods, and tools (thinking you know the "right" answer and the "right" way to do it)

- coaching toward your solutions

- environmental distractions like your phone, people nearby, and so on

- thinking about unrelated things (e.g., what happened before the meeting or thinking about something that needs to happen after the coaching session)

What to do if you are not being focused. Don't be afraid to pause the conversation and reestablish focus. If you lose focus, you can simply acknowledge it to the person being coached:

- I missed that last point. Could you repeat that?

- I feel like we are not on the same page. Can we revisit the focus of this conversation?

Take the time to create an environment that supports being focused—scheduling a meeting in a quiet place, putting away your cell phone, turning off your computer monitor, or sending your calls to voice mail.

Coaching people whose focus is too narrow or too broad. We have observed that there are usually three situations with the people we coach: people with a focus that is too narrow, people with a realistic focus, and people who have a focus that is too broad. Each of these cases requires a slightly different coaching approach.

Questions you can ask to help a person narrow their focus:

- Of the things you listed today, where would you like to start?
- You have mentioned several things. Which is most important? Which one is most urgent?
- What can we do today that will put you where you want to be tomorrow?
- What can we focus on that will be most beneficial?

Questions you can ask to help a person broaden their focus:

- That is one solution. What other things could you consider?
- What are some of the other things that will be impacted by this decision?
- If you knew you could not fail, what would you do?
- Could there be more to this that you are not currently considering?

Example

During a performance review, I gave a person some feedback they did not agree with. It was a suggestion on how they could be more effective. They became a little defensive and a little emotional about the suggestion. Instead of backing off and shying away from the emotion, I stayed focused on the behavior and helped that person consider how their behavior plays out in the workplace. When the conversation ended that day, the person was not in a place of owning the behavior.

A few weeks passed, and the person approached me to say that maybe there was some truth in what I was saying. They mentioned that someone else had a similar conversation with them after our discussion. At that point, they were ready to own their behavior and focus on improving how they were being perceived, not on defending their reputation.

—Coach Kevin

When we are coaching people there will be times when the person needs time to process the things we are discussing with them. Allow time and space for people to think during and after the coaching session. This processing time often results in self-discovery and increased self-awareness.

Reflection Questions

What does staying focused look like for you?

_____

_____

What will you be focused on during a coaching conversation?

_____

_____

How can you make sure that you are creating an environment that supports focus for you and the person being coached?

_____

_____

What is your recovery plan if you or the person being coached loses focus?

_____

_____

On a scale of 1–10 with 1 being "needs a lot of work" and 10 being "no work needed," how would you rate your ability?

- To stay focused on the person _____
- To stay focused in the conversation _____
- To stay focused on the coaching engagement_____

What will you need to do to improve your ratings?

- Internally (within yourself, your think/attitudes/beliefs/ habits)
- Externally (changes needed within your work environment to facilitate improvement)

Who can give you feedback on your ability to maintain focus in your day-to-day operations and specifically during conversations?

_____

_____

Capture additional thoughts and big ideas in the journal section in the back of the book.

Other related words: Accountability, Goals, Feedback, Emotions

GOALS & GOAL SETTING

Goal: a purpose, or something that you want to achieve
Goal Setting: the process of deciding what you
want to achieve or what you want someone
else to achieve over a particular period

—Cambridge Dictionary

COACHING IS FOCUSED on the future and looking forward to some type of future state. This future state may be expressed in hopes or dreams. When a person writes those dreams down, puts a plan together to achieve them, and incorporates timelines and deadlines, those dreams then become goals. In coaching, we are supporting the person's work toward something of value to them and the organization.

In the workplace, employees need direction to the extent that they need to know the objectives of the organization and how their tasks and activities support the achievement of the mission of the organization. John B. Miner states, "One of the principles of goal setting is that it helps a person to focus their attention and set priorities."[5] When you are coaching employees, setting goals is an

---

5   John B. Miner, *Organizational Behavior 1: Essential Theories of Motivation and Leadership* (New York: Routledge, 2015).

effective strategy in helping them to focus their time and energy in the right direction. Setting goals gives a person a target, something to point their tasks and activities toward. In the workplace, the focus will generally be on meeting performance goals, achieving results, and professional development.

Goals help establish milestones for achievement and a way to mark successes. There are some jobs where people get caught in an endless cycle of tasks and activities, and they lose motivation to do their jobs. To combat times when work seems like a continuous flow of tasks and activity, being intentional about setting daily and weekly goals can help a person experience success in their work. Helping a person understand how to manage their motivation by setting goals that are realistic for their type of work and working toward those goals will give them a sense of achievement. This sense of achievement can help them stay engaged in the workplace. Goals also help people with clarity and give an employee a sense of knowing they are doing the right things and contributing to the organization.

Setting goals gives you a blueprint for accountability. A plan with clear goals helps an employee make a commitment to certain actions and behaviors. Having the goal gives you a place to start the conversation about performance. When coaching a person to establish clear goals, you should also include plans on how to track progress and when to schedule follow-up conversations. We would suggest that you document this in some way either in an email or a shared document. Writing the goals and commitments down is a best practice for accountability and follow-up. When objectives are not being met, you can go back to the goals and evaluate the situation and consider if the right behaviors are being practiced to achieve those goals. When coaching people about their goals, ask the person questions about barriers to achieving their goals. You can also ask questions about being consistent and practicing the behaviors necessary to achieve the goals.

Having goals in place also help to get a person back on track if they have lost focus on what they should be doing each day. Goals help employees understand that others are literally counting on them to do their parts in moving work forward. Goals can help people understand that when they do their part and reach their goals, it allows others to do their jobs in a more efficient way.

When coaching employees, there will be two main areas of focus: goal setting performance goals and career development goals. The two can be closely related, however, they are not the same.

Performance Goals

Performance goals are usually about producing results, tasks, and activities to get the work done and achieve the goals of the organization. These performance goals should be aligned with organizational goals. Alignment with organizational objectives helps people see how their work contributes to the success of the team and organization. And it helps them see their work as relevant.

In most production environments, establishing performance goals are usually based on tangible outcomes. As we move into work where more people are paid for what they know and how they analyze information (knowledge workers), setting performance goals can be challenging. What does the outcome of knowledge work look like? Should a person be evaluated on quantity or quality? This is where leadership must invest the time in collaborating with employees to determine what goals should look like.

Career Goals

Career goals are about the person and their aspirations for their career and may include things such as building skills or acquiring knowledge, competing for different jobs or promotions, and achieving career/job satisfaction. Employees should have goals that support them in becoming who they want to be.

As the leader, investing the time to talk about performance goals and career goals will show employees that you not only care about the work, but you are interested in their success as well. This can even be at times when their goals might mean considering other responsibilities, switching to a different position, or even finding a new role at another organization.

For people to have ownership of a goal, they should have some say in the goal itself, or in how the goal can be achieved. Encourage people to adopt a structured approach to setting goals. One model is making SMART goals. SMART: specific, measurable, action-oriented, realistic and time-bound. Most people have heard of SMART goals. When coaching, we would encourage you to consider this acronym as you are working with your employees to set performance and career development goals.

When setting goals, be sure the person's goals are challenging yet attainable. If goals are realistic, they provide motivation to the person. If they are unattainable, at some point the goals can create frustration and discouragement. Using the SMART approach will help create goals that are comprehensive and give a person the opportunity to experience success.

There are outcome-based goals and behavioral goals. When coaching, consider setting goals based on behaviors instead of outcomes. An employee is responsible for their attitude, effort, and focus. They cannot always produce a specific outcome. Help employees establish goals that are based on the behaviors within their control. When a person focuses their energy on consistency and practicing the preferred behaviors, the desired outcomes are more likely to be achieved.

Tips

Make goals visible. Studies show that people who write down their goals are more likely to achieve them. Some examples of how people can do this:

- When a person has a goal, encourage them to write it down. Encourage them to write it on a sticky note and post it in a place they can see it.

- For organizational goals, make posters and put them up in the office. Include the goal on a prominent place on the company's intranet site.

Prioritize goals. "When everything is a priority, nothing is a priority."[6]

- All goals don't hold the same level of importance. Be sure to prioritize goals that have the most impact over goals with minimal impact.

- When setting goals, employees should understand the priorities of the organization and prioritize their individual goals to align with the priorities of the company.

Limit number of goals to three to five. Resist the urge to have six or more goals for any performance period of twelve months or shorter. Too many goals reduce a person's ability to focus effort. This can be modified based on the length of the performance period and should align with organizational plans and objectives.

Explore performance struggles. When you see people having performance struggles in the workplace, pause and consider what could be causing this struggle. Ask yourself these questions:

Performance Focused Questions

---

6   Karen Martin, *The Outstanding Organization: Generate Business Results by Eliminating Chaos and Building the Foundation for Everyday Excellence* (New York: McGraw-Hill Education, 2012).

- Does the employee have the right goals?

- Do they have them written down?

- Was the SMART model applied to the goal?

- How is this person measuring success?

- Do they know what the key behaviors are to accomplish their tasks?

- Have they lost focus and need help refocusing?

- Is the person investing the right amount of energy on the right types of work?

- Do they understand how their work contributes to the success of the team and organization?

Career Focused

- What is this person's potential?

- What type of development do they need to reach that potential?

- What are their career aspirations?

- Do they have a plan to reach their career potential?

Example

When I was working at a company and we were receiving work that came through the mail, there was a person on my team who would finish all of the work she received each day. When we switched to an online system and the work started coming into queues, she could not finish all of the work that came in the queues each day. This was a huge source of frustration, and this very competent person started to struggle with her work and how she felt about her work production. One of the reasons she was struggling was because she never felt a sense of making progress or being able to finish her tasks.

I had to help her rethink how she approached her work. We had to change the way she set her goals, instead of her goal being to finish each day. We worked together to determine what would be a realistic amount of transactions she could complete in a normal day. We then set goals to make these new standards her target. We also talked about managing the things within her control. She could not control the quantity and speed that work came into the systems; she could only control her focus and her effort. We also agreed on what the new measure for success in her role would be. Anytime she met or exceeded those goals, she would consider that a success. This new approach gave her a better sense of accomplishment. Helping her establish SMART goals helped her adjust to the new way of working.

—Coach Kevin

Reflection Questions

How can I increase my practice of good goal setting habits?

_____

_____

How can I support people in their goal setting?

_____

_____

When is the last time I invested time in learning about current goal setting methodologies?

_____

_____

On a scale of 1–10 (1 being terrible and 10 being amazing)

- How am I balancing performance goal setting with career goal setting? _____
- How consistent am I having timely goal setting and follow-up meetings with my team? _____

How can I be more effective in goal setting?

_____

_____

Who should I start having a career conversation with on my team?

_____

_____

Capture additional thoughts and big ideas in the journal section in the back of the book.

Other related words: Accountability, Expectations, Habit

HABITS

"SUCCESSFUL PEOPLE ARE simply those with successful habits," said Brian Tracy (author of *Daily Habits of Successful People*). Most of our clients hire us as their coaches because they want to be more success-ful as a leader. Once we help them determine what success looks like for them (which by the way is not so simple to define), we then help them identify those things that will make them that successful leader. In other words, we help identify the personal habits that they would need to accomplish their goal.

Author John Maxwell states you can determine the outcome of your success based on your daily habits.[7] Habits form who we are—how we show up in the world. In his book, *The Power of Habit*, Charles Duhigg talks about how our brains are constantly scanning for patterns they can turn into habits. Habits free up our minds to do other things—they save time. Our brains like habits because of

---

7   "Today Matters," johnmaxwell.com, January 15, 2014.

their efficiency and predictability. The efficiency and predictability of habits help to conserve our brain's energy and focus capability, which is in limited supply. One thing to note: as much as our brains like habits, they do not differentiate between good and bad habits. The brain loves patterns, and as soon as it identifies a pattern, it will begin to form a habit without regard to whether it is a good or bad one. Habits are powerful—they can be powerfully good or powerfully bad.

Here's an example of a powerful habit:
Let's say it is a workday, and it is just about quitting time. You wrap up the last email, straighten your work area, pull out your keys, and move toward the door. Once in your car, you turn on the ignition and radio and pull out. The next thing you know, you're pulling into your driveway. Then you have this startling, and a little scary, realization—you don't remember much about the drive home. You wonder if you stopped at the stop sign? Did you run any lights? You literally arrived at home without being fully present minded during the drive. What happened? Your brain recognized the pattern (email, work area, keys, car), and then the habit kicked in—driving home just like you do five days a week, every week.

Now to show how powerful that habit is let's look at this example:
You're at work, and just before quitting time, you get a call from your spouse asking you to stop by the cleaners. You make a verbal mental note to self: *Don't forget the cleaners.* You wrap up your last email, straighten your work area, pull out your keys, and move toward the door. Once in your car, you turn on the ignition and radio and pull out. The next thing you know, you're pulling into—no, not the cleaners—your driveway. How did that happen? It's not that you just forgot; your brain recognized your usual end-of-the-workday pattern, and the powerful habit of driving home kicked in.

Habits create routine, order, and efficiency in our lives. It doesn't look the same for everybody. The routine, order, and efficiency are determined by our choices and decisions. Once we have formed a habit, our brains are very resistant to changing or stopping that habit. The key is to form good habits, right? So how do we do that?

- Define the desired habit in detail. What would you be doing differently? How would you know if it has become a habit?

- Answer the *why*. It must be a habit that *you* really want.

- Start small. Pick one thing. Example: You want to create a habit of coaching. That is a very broad habit; it has many pieces to it. Pick one thing that a good coach has a habit of doing—let's say, listening more than telling. Pick one thing that you could start doing to listen more. Perhaps that first small thing could be a habit of not interrupting people to give your opinion. Once you have created the habit of not interrupting, move to the next piece.

- Make your habit specific and measurable.

- Create a commitment strategy. Who will you be accountable to? Who could support you? What resources do you need in place?

- Create a routine that will support your habit.

> **Tips**
>
> **Commit to the time.** It's going to take time to create a habit. Research studies show that it can take from 60 to 360 days to make a habit stick. Stay the course. Why stay the course? Habits can save and/or give us more discretionary time
>
> **Plan to fail.** Forgetting or getting off-track has no measurable impact on your success. You just make any needed adjustments and get back on track.
>
> **It is a process.** Create and be committed to the process

Measure behaviors. Measure success by the behavior changes that support your desired habit. An example: The habit you are working on is listening more effectively. A behavior change would be not interrupting people while they are speaking.

Lean into your motivation. We have a limited amount of motivation. Creating a habit can reduce your need for motivation to do that particular task. You then can utilize your limited motivation in other areas that need attention.

Celebrate. The brain recognizes when something is important to you, and it will reinforce its acceptance of that new habit. So celebrate big and small wins!

Example

I had a leader approach me after attending a coaching workshop that I had facilitated. In the workshop, we had discussed how difficult it was for some people to let go of the habit of being the go-to problem solver, especially if you considered yourself to be a hard-wired problem solver. He stated he saw value in being a coach and wanted to create the habit of using a coach approach rather than his natural tendency to problem solve all the time. We talked through what that would be like for him and why it was important to use more of a coach approach. He created a description of what being a coach versus the problem solver would look and sound like. It was a fairly broad description, so I challenged him to choose a small first step toward being the coach that he had described.

After several discussions, he decided he wanted to have a habit of asking a question first instead of launching into his problem-solving routine. We discussed all the barriers and triggers that he would need to be aware of and how to address them. He came up with his plan and embarked on his journey to create a coach approach to problem solving. He checked in regularly and confessed he failed often, but he did have a few successes. There were times he wanted to give up because it was just easier to do what was natural to him. We celebrated small wins along the way. He made adjustments to his approach and stuck with it. If you ask him, he will tell you that it took him about six months to really create the habit. And he said what made him successful was having a plan, being accountable, and being okay with failing.

—Coach JoAnn

Hopefully one of your goals is to be a better coach (that's why you are reading this book, right?). Here are some suggestions/questions/resources to consider:

- Define for yourself what a better coach means to you. It may be helpful to talk this through with a coach. Having a coach throughout the process could help with accountability and serve as a role model for you.

- A resource that could be helpful is a book by Charles Duhigg, *The Power of Habit.* It can provide support for your habit journey.

- Pick one characteristic/trait that you want to work on. Remember that being a coach is too broad for your brain to seriously consider. Working on one trait at time can lead to an eventual string of changed habits.

- Be okay with starts and stops. You will probably make several adjustments. Your brain prefers the habits it already has, so don't expect your brain to be cooperative. But with every do over or restart, it signals to your brain that this is important.

- Once you get that first trait/characteristic as part of your habit, pick another one. For some people an amazing thing happens—they find it doesn't take as long to add the next habit!

Just as you did not become a leader overnight, becoming a leader-coach will take time and good habits.

Reflection Questions

What habit would you like to create? Why?

_____

_____

What is going to be your biggest roadblock/barrier? Why?

_____

_____

What is one thing you could do to start the process?

_____

_____

What is one trait/characteristic of coaching that you would like to be a habit?

_____

_____

Capture additional thoughts and big ideas in the journal section in the back of this book.

Other related words: Barriers, Focus, Presence

INTEGRITY

*The practice of being honest and showing a
consistent and uncompromising adherence to strong
moral and ethical principles and values.*

—Oxford Living Dictionary

DURING A LEADERSHIP workshop, a group of leaders was asked to define integrity. After hesitating and stumbling over their words, they shared that they knew what it was—they just didn't know how to say what it was. If a leader doesn't have it, then they find it impossible to respect that leader. We have found that this is not unusual. Integrity is a value that consistently ranks high for leaders, but leaders find hard to define.

Oprah Winfrey once said that "real integrity is doing the right thing, knowing that nobody's going to know if you did it or not." Here's the thing. As a leader, you are being watched. Even when you think you are not, you probably are. And if you don't demonstrate integrity, it is likely that neither will your employees.

What do leaders who have integrity do to show it?

- Even when it's difficult or unpopular, they stand up for what they believe in.

- Instead of being certain that they are always right and everyone else is always wrong, they consider other's points of view. They understand the importance of gaining multiple perspectives.

- They have learned to recognize and manage their biases. Yes, their biases. We all have them. Biases are influenced by our cultural backgrounds and personal experiences. They can impact our decisions without us even knowing it.

- They show courage and own their mistakes. And when appropriate, they apologize.

- They treat others fairly and communicate respectfully.

- They challenge their assumptions by asking questions and enhancing their self-awareness.

- They give credit when it's due.

- They are authentic and transparent in word and deed.

Just like coaches, leaders maintain confidentiality. We can bet that there is information that you have that you will not share. Leaders are privy to information that others are not. This could be business information or personal information about their employees and colleagues. The sharing of confidential information is the quickest way to erode trust and destroy credibility. There may be times when a leader has an obligation to share information. An example of this is if the organization's code of conduct policy has been violated. In these cases, a leader must be honest and transparent about their obligation.

An important part of being a leader is coaching and mentoring other leaders. Developing others, including potential leaders, is a responsibility that often falls to the bottom of the priority list or is even forgotten. To be able to provide a safe space for coaching others, showing you are trustworthy and have integrity is imperative. No one will let themselves feel vulnerable if they do not feel like they can trust your integrity. And if they cannot be vulnerable, it will be more difficult to dig deep and support them in reaching their potential. When identifying potential leaders, integrity is a key value that you should expect. It is foundational to leadership. It is a deal breaker. If someone does not demonstrate integrity, leadership should not be an option.

Tips

Consistency is key. When describing the true mark of leadership, Brian Tracy, a motivational speaker and self-development author, says, "There can be no exceptions to honesty and integrity. Integrity is a state of mind. It is not situational."[8] You don't turn it on and off.

Identify your biases. Biases are typically demonstrated as being prejudicial, close-minded, or unfair. They can be innate or learned. Being aware of your biases is vital to being able to manage them.

Support others in solidifying and demonstrating integrity. The most important way to do this is by modeling integrity. Make it part of your team culture, set clear expectations, and make sure there are consequences for unethical behaviors.

Evaluate how you are doing.

- Who is in your circle that you trust to give you feedback? Maybe a mentor or your peers. Ask your team how you are doing.

- Look and listen for clues. What are others telling you about how they are perceiving you? They might not be telling you verbally. Are they physically reacting to what you say through non-verbal communications? Are they avoiding you? What is your intuition telling you?

- Check your intention. Is an agenda driving your behavior? Are you using manipulation to get what you want?

---

8   "The Importance of Honesty and Integrity in Business," briantracy.com.

Example

Coach Debby shared the following:

What not to do:

A leader realizes that an order they placed had incorrect information and therefore would be delayed. They decide to not share their mistake and let the shipping company take the blame.

What to do:

In a management meeting, a leader is given credit for an idea that was not their idea but one of their team member's ideas. The leader acknowledges how good the idea is and where the idea came from by sharing the team member's name with their colleagues. They also go back and recognize the team member for their contribution.

Reflection Questions

How do you define integrity?

_____

_____

How do you demonstrate your integrity?

_____

_____

Who are potential leaders who have integrity that you could coach and/or mentor?

_____

On a scale of 1 (needs work) to 10 (good at this), rate your ability to do the following:

- Create a team culture of integrity   ____
- Set clear expectations   ____
- Give consequences for unethical behavior   ____

What can you do to raise these scores?

_____

_____

What are your biases?

_____

_____

How will you evaluate how you are doing with integrity?

_____

_____

Capture additional thoughts and big ideas in the journal section in the back of this book.

Other related words: Culture, Trust

INTENTION

An idea or plan of what you are going to do or say

—Collins Dictionary

Have you ever had to explain your intentions, or have you made the statement "That was not my intention"? Maybe you have questioned other people's intentions? We make statements like "I'm not sure I fully trust his intentions," or "Oh, I hear their words, but I'm not sure they really mean them." Perhaps we say, "I will just wait and see." We've all met people that we just *knew* their intentions were not good. Out antennae go up, and then our guard shield moves into place. If people do not believe that our intentions are good, they will be resistant. It doesn't matter if we believe our intentions are good—what matters is what the other person believes. For example, you may think that your intentions are obvious when you are trying to get someone to improve their performance. The person on the receiving end of your intentions may think that your intention is to get them fired. Our brain's innate negativity bias (this is part of our brain's survival mechanism) is continually scanning for bad news. So if there is not a strong, trusting relationship, your intentions can be misinterpreted.

Good intentions are imperative to a coaching relationship (really, any relationship) because they build trust. And as we have stated often, trust is foundational to a coaching relationship. When people believe we have good intentions, they feel safer and more supported. They are more open to being influenced by you because they trust your intentions.

> ### Tips
>
> **You are in control.** You are in control of your intentions. It's up to you how you show up. Knowing your intentions will help create the plan/goal. Your intentions define how you will engage others in the plan/goal.
>
> **Ask yourself questions.** When you are concerned about how someone may interpret your intentions, ask yourself these questions:
>
> - What are my intentions for myself? How do I want to show up? Am I operating within my core beliefs? How is this impacting my behavior?
> - What are my intentions for the team? Organization? Issue?
> - What are my intentions for the person? What do I want for this person? How do I feel about them?
> - What outcome is needed? This can be harder to answer than one would think. Sometimes, we can get tunnel vision about the person and lose sight of the issue or project. Get clear about the needed outcome.
>
> **Be honest.** Be completely honest about your intentions. This takes real self-reflection and a willingness to get straightforward feedback.
>
> **State your intentions.** Be ready to state your intentions. Don't assume that people know what your intentions are. We cannot control what others are thinking, nor do we know all their past

experiences that can impact how they interpret our words and actions. Stating your intentions can potentially clear up any assumptions that they may have and/or give you an opportunity to answer questions that may have not occurred to you. People can see through a leader's veiled attempts to claim, "This is not about me." Don't mislead others about your intentions. Be honest even when you are being self-serving.

Example

I was assigned to coach a new-to-the-role leader. He had been a project lead on many high-profile projects and had just been promoted to his first formal supervisor role. He was excited about the new position and had outlined several goals that he wanted to accomplish with his new team. We talked about the importance of getting to know his team and operating out of his core beliefs. Although he was saying he understood the importance of understanding team dynamics and getting to know each person on the team, it was fairly apparent he was most interested in getting the job done quickly, efficiently, and perfectly.

After a couple of months, he was surprised to find out that a couple members of his team had complained to his boss about him. He stated he felt betrayed and confused. The team had completed all their projects perfectly and they were humming along. As we talked, I asked him what his intentions had been toward each of his team members. His first response was "to make them part of the best team ever!" What he discovered in our conversation is that he had had very few one-on-one conversations with his team. He also realized that he had been treating the team more as a tool; a means to an end. When asked how he thought the team and individuals may have interpreted his intentions, he wasn't sure, but he wanted to find out.

Over the next few weeks, he met individually with each team member to discuss how they saw him as a leader and how they had interpreted his intentions. His findings were sobering to him. The team thought his intentions were self-serving. I think it is important to note that this leader was willing to be vulnerable and did a good job of providing a safe environment for his team to talk. That doesn't always happen. He was able to turn the situation around because he was willing to examine his intentions and make changes.

—Coach JoAnn

Reflection Questions

Have you had your intentions misinterpreted? What do you think caused the misinterpretation? What did you learn?

_____

_____

How do you check in with other's intentions?

_____

_____

How do you check in with your own intentions?

_____

_____

When coaching someone, why do you need to think about your intention?

_____

_____

Capture additional thoughts and big ideas in the journal section in the back of this book.

Other related words: Trust, Environment, Judgment

JUDGMENT

---

*The act of assessing and forming an opinion, notion
or conclusion about a person or situation or event*

—Vocabulary.com

Hey! Don't judge! We hear that often these days. Someone puts
something out to the world, and the world responds with judgment.
It makes it hard to be vulnerable when you know you will be judged.
What does judgment have to do with being a leader-coach? If you are
in a leadership position, you may see judging as part of your role. You
must use your judgment to make good decisions or choose between
one plan or another or one person over another.

Good leaders do have good judgment. The kind of judgment that
we will be discussing is the kind that can disengage, silence, or isolate
people. When people think they are being judged, especially by their
leader or a person of influence, trust is harder to establish and sustain.
It makes it harder for them to ask for help or to give input. Judgment
hinders growth—yours and that of those you lead. You may be won-
dering if you have made people feel like you are judging them. Ask
yourself if you do or have done things like this:

- Avoided certain people. Maybe you just couldn't find a connection with that person but, didn't seem to have a problem connecting with other people.

- Used language that could be considered offensive or hurtful by some. It could be a statement like "Well, that was a dumb thing to do."

- Made fun of a particular person or a group of people; maybe be disguised with "I'm just kidding."

- Held negative thoughts about someone. You don't say them out loud, but you definitely think them.

- Think that someone's behavior is just attention seeking. Perhaps it's that person who always seems to have to share their "better idea" and discounts your ideas.

- Felt the need to correct someone in the moment. You don't wait until they have finished explaining how or why they did something. Nor do you wait until you are in a private place to discuss it.

- Interrupted people. Maybe they are babbling on or you think you've heard enough to understand the situation.

If you identified some of those actions, you may be signaling to people that you are judging. It may not be your intention, but the impact feels like judgment. People are resistant to being coached by someone they think is judging them.

Judgment is a survival mechanism, something we do to protect ourselves. But when we have too much judgment, it has negative effects on our thoughts as well as our physical and mental health. And, it has the same effect on those we lead. We can develop strategies to minimize unhealthy and nonproductive judgment.

Tips

Be aware. Identify when you're judging. This requires some emotional intelligence (EQ). Take note of your thoughts and words that you speak. Notice how people respond to you.

Question your thoughts. It's natural to judge, but do you notice that you are often critical to specific people or under certain circumstances? Ask yourself why you are feeling/thinking those judging thoughts. Is it grounded in reality/facts? Then work to resolve the issue.

Cultivate your compassion. Some people say that compassion just isn't one of their strengths, but you can learn to be more compassionate by deciding that you will. There are plenty of resources that can help you cultivate your compassion. Work on your compassion. One exercise that supports building your compassion is to listen. Don't interrupt. Don't problem solve. Just be quiet. When you do speak, make statements of affirmation or concern.

Get better friends. Don't hang around other people who are overly judging. This applies to personal and professional friends. You know the old saying, "Birds of a feather flock together!" Find another more positive, caring flock. Check in with people you trust and that know you. Tell them you're working on being less judgmental. What have they noticed? (Don't ask your very judgmental friends.)

Look for the positive. Try to say some positive things about others every day. If you are leading a team or working with a group of people, take time to notice things that each of them do well and then tell them. Don't forget to say positive things to yourself.

Identify your triggers. Remember that judging sets limitations on you and others. When you fall into the unhealthy and nonproductive trap of overly judging, take note of it. Try to identify the trigger and work on that. Ask someone to hold you accountable.

Example

Sometimes, we are not aware that our words and actions can sound like judgment. I experienced a leader who had moved up through the ranks as he would say. He knew everybody's job (so he thought) because he had done it at some point. He did have a wealth of knowledge, but he was not very good at learning from others. If someone suggested a different approach or a new idea for a project/problem, this leader often said, "Well, that's not how I would do it," or "Don't come to me later when it all falls apart." Of course, this would cause some to abandon their idea or solution and ask for his recommendation.

He "joked" around with some of his team members about their ethnicities. "All in good fun," he said. What was ironic was that this leader complained about how his team wouldn't take initiative or take the lead. It was often suggested to him that his team may not be very responsive because of some of his statements that could be interpreted as condescending and judgmental. He did not grasp the impact that his words had and would rebuff any suggestion for change with his usual, "I just call it like I see it. People are just too sensitive these days."

For years, this leader was given a pass because "That's just how he is. He doesn't mean any harm" was the general attitude by his leadership. As new leadership moved in, they became aware of this particular leader and the negative employee-opinion surveys. There was a concerted effort made to help this leader become more emotionally intelligent. He wasn't a bad person, and he was a great resource to the organization. His team praised his knowledge and hard work.

Eventually, his intellectual capital could not offset the need for him to change his approach to interacting with his team, and he was given the opportunity to retire. What made this an even sadder ending was that he left the organization feeling rejected and embittered by the judgment he said he felt. Yet, he was unable to admit and own how his own judgments and actions contributed to his early exit.

—Coach JoAnn

As leader-coaches, we must be aware of and manage that overly critical, judging voice in our head. It can become a habit that we no longer notice just like the example above. Don't become a victim of your own judgments. A suggestion that may help you dig into this a little deeper is our chapter on emotions and emotional intelligence. Check it out.

Reflection Questions

When have you noticed that you were being overly judgmental? What was the circumstance? At what point did you notice?

_____

_____

What words/phrases do you need to delete from your conversations?

_____

_____

How can you hold yourself accountable to not be judgmental? What is one thing that you can do right now?

_____

_____

Capture additional thoughts and big ideas in the journal section in the back of this book.

Other related words: Trust, Environment, Intention, Language, Emotional Intelligence, Safety

LANGUAGE

A system of conventional spoken, manual (signed),
or written symbols by means of which human beings,
as members of a social group and participants in its
culture, express themselves. The functions of language
include communication, the expression of identity,
play, imaginative expression, and emotional release

—Encyclopedia Britannica

Do you remember when you were young and you would say, "Sticks and stones may break my bones, but words will never hurt me"? Now that you are grown, you know that is not true. In fact, there are studies that show that people can overcome physical abuse and never overcome verbal abuse. We carry those words with us deep in our hearts and deep in our minds all our lives. Our words have power.

Language is one way to build safety for others. Be aware of your judgments and learn to acknowledge them and put them aside. If people feel judged, they will not hear what you have to say, trust will erode, and you will have no influence. If you have no influence, results will suffer.

Language can also affect others' perceptions of you. We work with leaders who will tell us how they want to show up, and then they get feedback regarding how others perceive them. Working on your emotional intelligence and being aware of areas you might need to work on can be valuable information. Often, there is a mismatch between a leader's vision and their words and actions. It holds them back from getting the outcomes they want.

The bottom line is that your language matters. Words can have an impact on your ability to build trust with others. It can let you get to know someone and for them to get to know you. It sets the environment—whether positive or negative. We know it can be hard to find what you believe are the right words. Let go of the idea that there are perfect words. Reflect on the words you are using and how you are using them. Are you coming across the way you want?

The language you use represents who you are as a leader. Pay attention to your words, how you make others feel with your language, and watch for clues for how you are being perceived. This is information that you can use to determine if your actions and intentions are aligned.

Tips

The following information is tips that we have come across over the years. It is easy to build bad habits around language. The tips are for you and also for you to share with the people you lead to maximize their power of language.

Stay away from weasel words. For all of the English language geeks out there (just like us), the phrase *weasel words* comes from a short story by Stewart Chaplin titled "Stained Glass Political Platform," published in *The Century Magazine* in 1900. That's how long it's been around! Weasel words are words that give the perception that you are not confident or competent.

- Replace weak words like "I think" and "I feel" for stronger options such as "I'm confident," "I'm convinced," and "I believe." These changes can make a difference in how a message is perceived.

- Using hedge words like *just*, *probably*, or *kind of* can reduce your credibility.

- Tag lines such as "Right?" and "Don't you think?" sound like you are asking for reassurance for what you are saying and do not instill confidence in your message.

- Have you ever recorded a conversation that you were participating in and then listened to it? That can be an eye-opening experience. We often add words that bring no value to what we are saying or writing. Words like *okay* and *so*.

- Absolutes are words like *always, never, best*, and *worst*. They are throwaway words. When you tell someone, "You are always interrupting me," people are going to feel the need to defend themselves, and we can guarantee that they are going to come up with that one time they didn't interrupt you and discredit your entire message.

Be intentional with your choice of words. Sometimes, being more thoughtful about your choice of words can make a world of difference.

- Try replacing *but* with *and*. It will open people up. For example, instead of saying, "You are very good at answering questions, but you need to work on your opening statements," could you say, "You are very good at answering questions, and if you keep working on your opening statements, your presentations will be even better"?

- When sharing information that you do not want to turn into a debate, use language such as "it appears to me" or "in my opinion."

- Different words mean different things to people. For example, if you say you want something done "later that day," do you mean three o'clock or midnight?

In addition to the words you use, things like inflection, tone, and body language can make a difference.

- "Uptalk" is when you end statements with upward inflections to make them sound like questions. It gives others the impression that you are not sure of what you are saying or that you would change your opinion easily if the person you are talking to does not agree. It shows a lack of confidence and assertiveness. Uptalk is prevalent among young women.

- Have you ever asked someone how their day was, and you get a "fine" in response that, based on the irritated tone and crossed arms that came with it, gives you the idea that their day was definitely not fine? This is a perfect example of how body language and tone makes a difference.

How can you help others with their language skills? In addition to your use of language, pay attention to the language that others are using. Their language can provide clues to what is going on with them and what is important to them. This is all great information to help you lead and coach.

- **Be curious.** Ask yourself: What do they mean by the words they use? Why are they using those particular words? Maybe they do not notice a certain word or phrase they have used a couple of times. Sometimes, you hear a word and your radar goes up.

- **Point out mismatches.** Sometimes, you may hear a mismatch. This is when something they say contradicts something else like a goal they have set, something they have said previously, or their actions. You will want to point out the mismatch and ask them about it.

- **Mirror their language.** Verbal mirroring is based on the work of psychologist and author Carl Rogers (1902–1987),[9] and relies heavily on listening closely and then using the speaker's vocabulary when responding. This technique creates a connection. People will say later that they felt heard and that they thought that this person listened to them. Using their language back to them, not parroting them or mimicking them but truly using their language, helps them connect and feel safer.

Example

I was a new leader with my first team. I was very excited about my new role. That excitement soon turned to frustration when my team started missing deadlines that I had set for them. I had been through new supervisor training and I felt that I was being clear and had set up an environment where my team could come talk to me if they thought they might miss a deadline. Some of the deadlines were for information that I needed for me to meet a deadline for my boss. My anxiety was growing.

I called my team together and I asked what was going on. They all denied they had missed deadlines. I started giving examples. Their response was: "you said you needed that at the end of the day" or "it was due later in the week." I did say I needed it at the end of the day and not all of them had met the deadline.

I took a deep breath and asked them each to write down what did "end of the day" and "later in the week" mean to them. I did the same and shared my thoughts. The end of the day to me was 5:00, which was the end of the workday. Later in the week

9   https://www.psychologytoday.com/us/blog/
here-there-and-everywhere/201101/6-amazing-things-carl-rogers-gave-us.

was no later than Thursday, so I had Friday to work on what I needed to do. Their response? We didn't know that's what you meant. Some felt end of day meant midnight. Others thought that later in the week meant end of the workday on Friday.

We had a great discussion and I learned a valuable lesson about the language I was using and how that language was not clear and carried my own assumptions.

—Coach Debby

We may think someone means one thing based on our experiences, our personalities, the culture we come from, and where we grew up. It may mean something completely different to others. Be aware of your language and how it might be misunderstood. Ask others for clarity on their language.

- What does that look like to you?
- What does that mean to you?

Reflection Questions

Consider your language patterns. Which habits would you like to break?

_____

_____

How will you break these habits and instill new habits?

_____

_____

Ask someone that you trust and who can hear your conversations, to give you feedback on your use of language. Who could that be?

_____

_____

As mentioned above, record yourself speaking and listen back to it. Make notes on what you notice and how you can improve those things. How can you support others with their use of language?

_____

_____

Capture additional thoughts and big ideas in the journal section in the back of this book.

Other related words: Culture, Curiosity, Environment, Feedback, Habit, Judgment, Messaging, Safety, Trust

LISTEN

To hear something with thoughtful attention:
give consideration: to be alert

—Merriam-Webster.com

ACCORDING TO VARIOUS studies, we can listen at a pace of nearly four times the rate at which we speak. Our rate of speaking is usually from 125–150 words per minute. Our rate of listening averages 600 words per minute. What this tells us is that we have ample time to listen and understand what a person is saying to us. Yet how often do we hear complaints that someone is not listening? Listening is one of the best ways to make a connection with someone we are coaching. We know that a strong connection promotes a more productive and transparent coaching relationship.

The purpose of listening is to better understand and support the person that you are coaching. You are listening to ask better questions. Often, new leader-coaches will voice concern that they are not sure which questions to ask. We believe, if you are truly listening, the next question will present itself.

Listening is not just about the words that are being spoken; it is also about listening beyond the words—what is being communicated through a person's choice of words, tone, body language, and what is *not* being said. When we really tune in to a conversation and listen with curiosity and without judgment, we gain a deeper understanding of the person. They in turn feel heard and are more willing to dig deeper.

> ## Tips
>
> **Be curious.** Get curious about why the person you are coaching used a specific word or phrase. What words are they emphasizing? Why are they choosing those words? What words are they repeating? Why did they pause for a long period of time? By being curious, you will give your brain a task that helps you stay focused on the person you are coaching.
>
> **What are they *not* saying?** Our choice of words is only part of the message. The rest of the message comes from body language and tone. In our chapter "Emotions and Emotional Intelligence," we are told to notice what is happening with others. Are they squirming in their chair? Is their face turning red? Has the rate of their speech increased? People say a lot with their bodies and tone. And so do you!
>
> **Identify and minimize distractions.** You will need to determine what distracts you and reduce those diversions. Is it the phone buzzing, people walking by? The chatter in your head or the problem solver in you that wants to speak?
>
> **Give Your Attention.** Be intentional about listening. Face the person you are coaching. Make eye contact. Get your head in the game by taking deep breaths, clearing your head of its to-do list. Remind yourself that listening is your most important role. If you are talking by phone, turn off or remove yourself from distractions.
>
> **Use Silence.** Ask a question and then get quiet. We used to think

that silence in a conversation was a bad thing. Actually, silence made us a little nervous. We have learned that silence is one of the best things you can offer. We need to become more comfortable with it. Silence provides time to reflect, time to really consider a question, and time to regroup and gather thoughts. Effective use of silence is a great tool whether in a one-on-one conversation or with a group. Silence says that we are willing to listen.

WAIT. As leaders we often think we don't have time to wait around on people to come up with their plan or give us an answer. People who are extroverted and love to help problem solve really struggle with this. I (Coach JoAnn) know that waiting is not one of my strengths. I am an extrovert. I love to talk. My biggest challenge as a new leader who desired to be a coach was listening. I struggled with disciplining myself to be quiet and really tune in to the person that I was coaching. A few months into my coaching, I took a class to enhance my coaching skills and talk with other leaders. It was in this class that one of the facilitators shared their story of struggling to stay quiet. She said she came up with the acronym WAIT. The acronym served as a reminder for her to wait and ask herself mentally the question, "Why am I talking?" If she didn't have a valid reason for interjecting or interrupting the person, she remained quiet. I put it to use at my next coaching session. I wrote WAIT at the top of my writing pad. When I had the urge to interject or interrupt the person I was coaching, I would glance at the acronym. It worked for me, so I am offering it to you if you are struggling with talking too much. Learn to use **WAIT**. Ask yourself: Why Am I Talking? Are you really listening or just waiting for your time to talk?

Example

As a teenager, my mom often told me that there was a reason that I was given two ears and just one mouth. Of course, I was much older before I fully understood her meaning. My mother was a great role model. People would seek her out. One of those who sought out my mom shared with me that they always felt like my mom really heard their heart. I asked my mom once why she thought so many people wanted to talk to her. Her response was simple: "Because I will listen." She taught me that one of the greatest gifts that you can give someone is to simply listen.

—*Coach JoAnn*

A good coach is an excellent listener. If you will discipline yourself to listen, our prediction is that you will be a sought-after leader.

If you are struggling to make a connection or having difficulty really listening to someone who reports to you and/or someone you are trying to coach, there are a couple of things you can do. To make the conversations more productive and transparent, try one of these questions:

- What would be most beneficial for us to talk about today?
- What do you think is getting in our way of having productive conversations?
- How could I be a better listener?

Once you ask the question, be silent! Listen! WAIT.

Reflection Questions

How good of a listener are you? How do you know? Ask others to give you feedback on their perceptions of your listening skills. Checking in with family, friends, peers/colleagues, and subordinates could give you great insight.

_____

_____

What is your biggest distraction to listening? What is one thing you could do to minimize it?

_____

_____

Would you say that you are a curious person? People who are curious tend to be more observant and will ask questions. How could you practice being more curious?

_____

_____

Identify an opportunity that you will practice listening. After the practice, reflect on how you did and how you can get better.

_____

_____

Capture additional thoughts and big ideas in the journal section in the back of this book.
Other related words: Culture, Questions, Curiosity, Silence

MESSAGING

---

*A communication containing some information,
news, advice, request, or the like, sent by
messenger, telephone, email, or other means*

—DICTIONARY.COM

MESSAGING IS USED to create clarity and help to move people forward. In many organizations, messaging is related to sharing company-wide information or having a cohesive internal or external communication strategy. That is not what we are referring to in this chapter. Messaging in coaching refers to sharing statements that include your ideas and insights and is a communication skill that allows you to interject new information into the discussion in an unbiased way.

Coaching is about helping people discover what is important to them and how they can take steps to get where they want to be with their performances, their careers, relationships, or personal lives. There are times when you need to share information that the employee does not have. You could share a personal or organizational perspective that the employee would benefit from knowing. Messaging is sharing information with people that broadens their perspective or gives them insight into things they are not aware of.

A message can be considered constructive feedback. When you share a message with someone, your intent should be clear to the person. Messaging is meant to help accelerate the person's discovery process and improve their performance in the future.

There are many instances when you can give an employee a verbal coaching message:

- **When they are stuck**. If a person is not making progress, if they are caught in a nonperforming loop, sharing a message could help them get on the right track or gain momentum in what they need to be doing.

- **When they have a blind spot.** There are times when people just don't see it. They have a blind spot, there is something that they are unaware of, and you can share information with that person and help them see a more complete picture. Messaging around a blind spot increases a person's awareness of other's perceptions of their behavior or other things they had not considered such as attitudes or thinking patterns.

- **When their behaviors don't match their stated desired outcomes**. This is when a person has a stated goal, but they are not doing the things they need to do to achieve their goal. There are even times when employees are doing things that are in direct conflict with achieving their goals.

- **When people ask for help or advice.** There will be times when the person you are coaching will get to a place where they want you to tell them what to do. The person may have exhausted their ideas or what they have tried did not work. They may not be able to see a way out and will ask for help. This is a good time to share your insight with that person.

Tips

Be truthful and kind to the person. You can deliver a tough message and do it in a way that is respectful and uplifting to the person. You want them to have a positive impression of receiving the message from you.

Make the message empowering. The receiver of the message should feel empowered by that message. It should be a message that is actionable and creates forward momentum for the person toward their goals.

Deliver it with empathy. Delivering a message is not about putting a person in their place or making them feel inferior. It is about giving them insight, uncovering a blind spot, helping them see untapped potential or equipping them with information to make better decisions.

Appropriate for the strength of your relationship. The stronger your relationship is with the employee, the more latitude you have to share your message. I would not walk up to a stranger and give them a message about how they came across at a board meeting. I would walk up to a twenty-year friend and share a message with them about how they may have stepped on some toes in the board meeting and why I think they should take a different approach if they want to influence the decision. You may not always be the person to share a message. If your relationship is not strong enough you may need to invest in strengthening the relationship or find another person with a better relationship with the person to deliver the message. Another approach may be acknowledging where your relationship is with the person, then asking them if you can share an observation with them. Based on their response you will know how to proceed. Either way, proceed with caution and good intent.

Practice Delivering Messages. Messaging is a skill, and it takes practice. When you feel the need to give someone a message, make sure you create the right environment, understand your relationship with the person, use language that is honest and kind, and deliver it to the employee as a gift or something to consider. Remember it is a message, not a command. Share in a way that will minimize adverse reactions:

- **Ask for permission.** Don't just blurt out your opinion of what you think someone should do. It should sound something like this:

  ○ "Bob, do you mind if I share an observation with you?"

  ○ "Sally, I have something I would like you to consider. Is it okay if I share a story?"

- **Share it as an option**. When giving a message, share it as an option that the person can accept, reject or modify. This is what it should sound like:

  ○ "Bob, there are multiple ways to resolve this. Have you considered this?"

- **Share it as an observation.** If you have observed the person's performance or behavior, share what you have observed. It should sound like this:

  ○ "The last time I saw you giving a presentation, I noticed you had a pocket full of change and you kept your hand in your pocket jingling the change. This behavior was distracting."

- **Tell or share a story.** A story is a way to share a message without coming straight out and saying it. Make it sound like this:

  ○ "Sally do you mind if I share a story?. I once was in a similar position as you. When I encountered this customer I realized, the most effective way to communicate with them was—"

  ○ Minimize the emotion and judgment in your message

- **Be Clear.** Do not distract from your message by including unnecessary emotions such as disappointment, anger, resentment, disgust, impatience, frustration, malice, or threat.

- **Allow Time for Processing.** After you deliver a message, give the person time to consider what you said. Don't gloss over it and move to the next thing. This is a good time to use silence effectively and wait until the person responds. Also be aware that they may accept, modify or reject a message.

Example

I told one of my friends I wanted to dramatically reduce the number of carbs that I was eating. I was sitting at her desk one day, and I told her, "I'm going to do this South Beach thing. I'm going to stop eating all of these carbs, and I'm going to really do this!"

A few days later, we had a business luncheon, and the menu was a sandwich buffet. As I got in the line, I was talking to all those around me, and I started fixing my plate. I started off at the sandwich buffet. I got a roll and a salad. I decided to make a sandwich. This day, the ciabatta looked so good. I think I had chips and a couple of cookies.

As I was walking toward the dining area with my loaded plate, I ran into my friend. She said, "Are you going to eat all of those carbs?" and just walked past me. I just stood there.

I thought, Do I really *need* all of these carbs? *I was able to hear and accept the message because the person saying it was not just a coworker but a close friend, and I trusted her intent.*

As I considered what was on my tray, I probably had every carb that was offered that day. I was surely behaving as if I did.

When I sat down with my tray, of course, none of the food tasted good. To me, this was the perfect example of a mismatch of stated intent versus actual behavior. While at her desk, I was saying one thing, but when I was preparing my plate, I was doing something else. My behavior did not match my stated goal.

—Coach Kevin

Reflection Questions

On a scale of 1 to 10 (1 "I am terrible at giving a message" to 10 "I am a pro")
How would you rate yourself on the skill of messaging? _____

What part of giving a message are you good at?

_____

_____

What part of messaging do you need to work on?

_____

_____

How can you be more kind and candid when delivering messages?

_____

_____

How can deliver your feedback and messaging in a way that moves a person forward?

_____

_____

What can you do today to deliver a message in a way it can be received?

_____

_____

Capture additional thoughts and big ideas in the journal section in the back of the book.

Other related words: Accountability, Feedback, Relationships, Resistance

MINDSET

A person's way of thinking and their opinions

—Cambridge Dictionary

Mindset is all about thinking. The way we think determines what we do, what we focus on, and the effort we give.

One of the biggest challenges in coaching is trying to change people's mindsets or ways of thinking. So our advice is *don't* try it. Instead of trying to change people's mindsets, help them expand their way of thinking to *include* different perspectives.

Some people have a fixed mindset, believing that their capacity to improve their performance is fixed or limited and cannot be improved. There are other people who have growth mindsets, and they believe their capacities to improve their performance in different aspects of their lives are dependent on acquiring more knowledge, more skills, and giving more effort. They believe they can get better. Some people are stuck in their limited thinking; others are open to new and limitless possibilities.

When coaching, there are two people's mindsets that are critical to the success of the coaching relationship: yours and the person being coached. What kind of mindset do you have as a leader-coach? What type of mindset does the employee have?

Our mindsets have been shaped by our life experiences. Through these life experiences, we have developed biases and paradigms that we hold to consciously and unconsciously. When you are coaching employees, understand that every individual has their own unique perspective of the world, and that includes what work means to them. When coaching, one of the things you may have to do is ask the employee questions that makes them aware of their mindset and how they are approaching their situation. In my experience, some people with fixed mindsets don't often perceive that they have fixed mindsets. They think, *This is just how the world is*, and, *This is how I am*.

To help someone expand their mindset, it will take time and intention on your part and theirs. Once a person is willing to consider that there are other possibilities, you can help them create plans and identify behaviors to help them move forward. If they have been having performance issues, they may feel like they are not in control and their situation is beyond repair. Through your leadership and coaching, you can help the person identify a path and set small, achievable goals as a way of demonstrating there is hope for them and potential for their performance.

When working with people who you think may have a fixed mindset, we would encourage you to listen to the responses to your questions: Are they blaming others? Do they not notice their roles in conflict situations? Do they only see problems or barriers? These may be clues that a person has a fixed mindset.

To help a person expand their mindset, they will need to be exposed to something new. Their current approach may be a habit as we discussed in the chapter on habits. When you are coaching an employee who has an unproductive mindset, there are four coaching strategies you can use to consider. The four strategies we recommend are: giving the person additional information, helping them try new behaviors, sharing others' experiences with them, and getting them a mentor.

- New information—sometimes, people think a certain way because they are basing their ideas and opinions on the information they have. If they can be exposed to additional information, they may change their mind.

- Facts—some people have fixed mindsets because they have been exposed to rumors and false narratives. They have bought into them, assuming they are the truth. The excuse that everyone else is doing this did not go away in middle school. You may have to pull out the data and have a discussion of the real metrics of a situation. There are times when seeing the hard numbers can help a person get a more accurate picture of what is going on and this may cause a shift in their mindset.

Small Behavior Changes

- When trying to get someone to adopt a new behavior, you may need to coach them as they consider trying a new behavior on a small scale. Even if they are not fully bought in, they could try the new behavior and then review the results. "Steve, try the new system for three days, and then we will talk about the pros and cons on day four."

- People's mindsets can be fixed because they are stuck in a paradigm or a way of thinking. Sharing a new approach or a different perspective can help a person expand their mindset.

Vicarious Experiences

- Sometimes, sharing a story of someone who made the change and is currently experiencing success can be a catalyst for someone expanding their mindset.

- Watching someone else do it. Some people will say, "I'll believe it when I see it." You may have to partner the reluctant person with someone who is proficient at the new behavior and has a growth mindset. This partnering experience can help them see that others are doing it, and this could expand their thinking to include the possibility that they could do it also.

When coaching, you may encourage the person to find someone who can be a mentor to them, preferably someone with a growth mindset. You could offer to introduce them to some potential mentors if you have people in mind. Mentoring relationships would help the employee build a different relationship other than the direct-reporting relationship they have with you. The mentor will be able to influence the person being coached in different ways.

Sometimes, an employee's mindset is being shaped by the people they are hanging around. You cannot tell them to get new friends, but through coaching, you can help them examine their relationships to consider if they have people in their lives who are influencing them in negative ways or in ways that do not support where they are trying to go.

Tips

Be respectful when discussing the person's mindset. Understand that this way of thinking may have been part of this person for a long time. It may be reflective of their family or culture, so don't be quick to judge the person's mindset.

Don't try to change the person. Don't try to change their mind. Only the employee can change their mind. You can help them expand their mindset to consider things outside of their current mindset. When you encounter an employee with a fixed mindset, don't immediately label the person as having a bad attitude. Consider that they have a reason for having this mindset. Take some time to get to know the person and inquire about their mindset.

Consider different things to broaden their perspective. Sometimes, people may not know there is another way. Most people don't wake up in the morning and say, "I am going to have a fixed mindset today." No matter what the person is thinking, they are doing that because it has been formed over time. They are operating inside of their worldview. Offer to help them have new experiences to shape and expand their worldview. You may not be able to change a person's worldview, but you could expand it and help them include other possibilities in their mindset.

Acknowledge their current mindset. When coaching someone who needs to adopt a different mindset, consider asking the person questions to help uncover the reasons they are having their current mindset. Explore why they have the current mindset. Get them to consider other possibilities. Ask them to come up with other options to their current way of thinking. Have them make a pro-and-con list of their mindset and the mindset you want them to adopt.

Give them other resources. Share books, articles, videos, or other tools to expand their knowledge base about different mindsets. There are some people who are open to expanding their mindset once they know of a better way. Give them time and space to self-discover and expand their worldview.

In this chapter, the focus has mostly been on helping others expand their worldview and adopt a growth mindset. If you find yourself in a place where you are stuck as a leader-coach, we would encourage you to apply the concepts from this chapter to yourself. We challenge you to consider learning more about growth mindsets, trying new behaviors, seeking enriching experiences outside of your comfort zone, and finding a mentor (most successful leader-coaches have people who coach them). Increasing your self-awareness about your mindset and overcoming your challenges will equip you with the knowledge, skills, and experiences you will need to support others.

Example

I had a coworker who had a competitive mindset. Having a competitive mindset can be good when it is focused on the competition. It can be a bad thing when it is focused on beating or showing up your teammates. This person had a tendency to compete with coworkers in an unhealthy way. They wanted to be seen, they wanted to be a superstar, and they wanted others to know it. The problem with this was the person was competing with coworkers and did things to promote themselves. The energy they were expending on outdoing others on the team should have been funneled into growing as a team, preparing for initiatives, and meeting the needs of clients.

This person worked with a leader who was able to provide them mentoring and coaching. Through the mentoring and coaching relationship, the employee was able to find their place on the team and started focusing on collaborating with their teammates versus competing with them. This collaborative mindset was modeled for the person, and the mentor supported them in their performance and customer successes. Their mentor worked with them and helped them experience what the results of collaboration looked like. Ultimately, the person learned the value of working together to meet the needs of the clients. They expanded their perception of success and understood that it was more important to meet the needs of the customer as a team. This gave our team more synergy and capacity to deliver on expectations. No one on the team had to be a superstar when we could be a team of all-stars.

—Coach Kevin

Reflection Questions

On a scale of 1–10 (1 being a fixed mindset and 10 being completely open to growth)
How would you rate your mindset? _____

How would you describe your mindset?

_____

_____

Do you have a growth mindset about your ability to become a better coach? How do you know?

_____

_____

In what part of your life do you need to expand your view of the world?

_____

_____

How can you shift from trying to change people's minds to expand their view of the world?

_____

_____

Capture additional thoughts and big ideas in the journal section in the back of the book.

Other related words: Focus, Change, Expectations, Resistance

PRESENCE

The state of being present and fully focused or involved in what is happening in the moment

—Yourdictionary.com

Have you ever tried to have a conversation with someone and realized that they were not really listening to you? You walk into your boss's office and ask to speak to him. He says yes, but he never looks away from his computer or only glances at you. Or an issue keeps popping up and you drop by a colleague's office to just blow off your frustration. Your colleague, instead of listening, starts telling you what you should do. How does that impact you? For many, it frustrates the heck out of them. We all have had this happen so much with some people that we no longer try to have any kind of conversation with them. Why bother? So what's happening when they do that? It is called lack of presence. They are not present. Everything about their body language, words, tone, and lack of interest tells you their presence is focused elsewhere. One thing is for sure—it's clear that they are not focused on you. It is important to note that listening is a big part of presence but listening is not the same as being present. You have to be present in order to really listen.

The world is one busy place. Everyone is busy, busy, busy. We wear it like a badge of honor. We are so busy that we fail to be present. A sign of a good leader-coach is their ability to be present with a person. Why is that important? Being present can impact how productive a conversation will be. Our full presence can be empowering to people. Being fully present tells a person that you value them. When you are present, you are watching body language, paying attention to tone, and looking and listening for clues and insight. Your questions and responses tell the person just how present you are. The more present you are, the more your questions and responses reflect what the person is trying to say or in some cases—what's not being said. Being fully present can have a very positive impact on people. It builds trust and rapport. When we feel heard, we feel connected. When we feel connected, we are more engaged.

Being present must be practiced and intentional. If we want our employees to be fully engaged, we must be fully present.

Tips

Distractions. Remove or leave the distractions. Turn away from your computer. Move away from your desk and put your phone on silent. Shut the office door if possible. Set aside whatever you were working on.

Shift. Shift your body and your thoughts toward the person that needs your attention. Remind yourself that they deserve your undivided attention.

Look. One way to let people know that you are listening is to look at them. Don't stare but make direct eye contact.

Engage. Ensure that they know that you are ready to engage with them:

Don't make statements like the following:

- *I'm really busy so I only have a few minutes.*

- *What do you need to talk to me about?*

Do make statements like these:

- *I'm glad to see you.*

- *What's top of mind for you today?*

Listen. Really focus and listen. Don't interrupt.

Don't be a clock-watcher. Stop constantly looking at your watch or the clock.

Affirm them. Recognize and affirm their emotions. Say things like these:

- *I can hear your frustrations.*

- *I can see that you are concerned.*

- *Sounds like you are happy with the results.*

Confirm. Let them know that you are hearing them. Repeat some of their words back to them. Example: Your employee tells you that he thinks something is screwed up with a report. Your question to the employee is, "What do you think is screwed up about the report?"

Thank them. Let them know that you appreciate the conversation and that you value their input.

Be up front. If you cannot be fully present because of other pressing priorities, ask to reschedule. It's okay to inform them that you have a certain amount of time, but it's important to give them options if possible. "Joe, I have a pressing deadline today. I can give you fifteen minutes now, or we can reschedule for tomorrow. What do you prefer?"

Example

I have always been a working mom—juggling a career, family, and home. It was all-consuming at times. One day, I picked up my four-year-old daughter from daycare and, as usual, rushed home to prepare dinner before her older brother had to leave for a game. My daughter chatted away in her car seat on the way home and then followed me to the kitchen as I was hurriedly preparing dinner. I was listening to her and uttering occasional words of affirmation and a lot of "oh, really" responses. In between her slight pauses, I was yelling instructions to my son, who was upstairs getting ready. She would stand as close as she could to me and tell me her stories. I admit that my thoughts were in a hundred different directions as she talked. This day, I felt a strong pull on my pants leg. When I looked down, I saw my daughter's big eyes looking up at me.

She said, "Mommy, you're not listening to me!"

I replied, "Oh, yes I am."

To which she replied, "No, you're not. I need you to listen with your eyes!"

That was a wake-up call to me about the importance of presence. My four-year-old daughter knew that I was not present. People deserve for us to be present.

When a leader-coach is fully present, they are completely focused and centered on what is happening in that moment. They are connected and concentrating on the person and/or the current conversation. Through disciplining the many voices in your head, the strongest one is the one that is saying, "This is the conversation/issue/person that needs your full attention right now."

Because you have decided to be present, you listen better and ask better, more productive questions. You will pick up nuances that could easily have slipped by you before. Problems get solved quicker. Most importantly, people feel heard and valued. And people who feel heard and valued give more of their discretionary energy.

—*Coach JoAnn*

Reflection Questions

Are you fully present when you are talking to someone? How do you know? How do they know you are?

_____

_____

What do you need to do to improve your presence with those you lead?

_____

_____

What gets in your way of being present? How can you better manage those things?

_____

_____

Capture thoughts and big ideas in the journal section of this book.

Other related words: Listen, Barriers, Intention, Focus

QUESTIONS

A sentence in an interrogative form, addressed to someone in order to get information in reply

—DICTIONARY.COM

SCIENCE HAS SHOWN that when a person is asking a question, much more of the brain lights up than when they are told to do something. A question seems to wake up the brain. By asking questions, you are supporting others in learning how to think strategically and to be empowered to get results. You are building their confidence to think critically, make decisions, and get things done.

You will hear us say this over and over in this book. Trust is the foundation for coaching, including asking questions. There are many factors that will play into how the person you are coaching receives your question. This includes your intention in asking the question, the tone you use, and the relationship you have with the person. Asking questions can make you feel vulnerable, but that is not a reason to stop asking them.

Jennifer Meiss, a midmanager at a Fortune 50 company says, "It's about knowing the person. There could be some history for a person around a particular questioning style or a specific question. In the past, when a leader asked them that question, it wasn't coming from a good place. So maybe it's from a good place now but unfortunately you are paying the price for the mistrust that came before. The relationship comes from more than one interaction. You don't develop trust in one conversation. You can lose trust in one conversation. It really is an investment. You learn so much if you just stop, listen and ask questions."[10]

What will asking questions get you? Asking questions has the potential to raise possibilities that people have never thought of, it may allow people to admit a barrier, like fear, that is holding them back, and it will help you gain insight into the person you are coaching. This is all information that you need to support others in moving forward.

Leaders assume that people come to them for the answer. Aren't leaders expected to have the answer? Admit it: it makes you feel important when people think you have the answer and can solve their problems. Step back and ask yourself if that's really what is happening. Maybe that was your strength before you became a leader? You were knowledgeable and good at what you did, which is probably what got you noticed. Here's the truth: giving the answer gives the illusion that things are moving forward. What you do not realize is that sometimes you are creating larger issues down the road. If you believe that asking questions hurts your credibility as a leader, you are missing the big picture. And the bottom line is it's not about you. It's about the people you lead.

> **Tips**
>
> **Consider the types of questions you are asking.** Your goal is to get the person you are coaching *talking*. Open-ended questions are questions that require more than a yes-or-no answer. You

---

10   *The Word on Coaching Podcast*, Season 2, Episode 1.

want to ask open-ended questions that are not leading to your answer or your agenda.

There could be times when asking a close-ended question can be helpful. Typically, this is when you are looking for clarification or commitment.

Be present and listen. When you are in the moment and really listening, you will be amazed at the clues you will pick up from the other person and how you will hear what they are saying and not saying. Trust that you will know what to ask.

Be curious. What did they mean by a word they used? Why did they sigh before they answered? What might be going on with them that you don't know? What is important to them?

It's okay to prepare. Although most opportunities for coaching are spontaneous, there will be some opportunities that are planned. Prior to the meeting, consider some questions you can ask to get the conversation started and make sure you are clear on the purpose of the conversation and your intended outcome.

Consider the person you will be talking to. What do you know about them? Are they more direct and like a fast pace? Or do they need some time to process what you are asking? Are they more results focused, or people focused? This information can help you coach them in a way that is both supportive and challenging.

Decrease the opportunity for frustration. Consider these suggestions:

- Be aware of your style. Is it what they need, or do you need to flex your style?

- State your intention. Make sure they understand the questions are for them, not you.

A tip from leaders who ask a lot of questions is that they tell their teams that they are inquisitive and they share where that comes from. They explain that they want to understand, learn, and move the work forward.

- Know when to limit the questioning.

Keep working on your questioning skills. We asked a group of leaders how they got better at asking questions. Here is what they told us:

- They "stole" questions from others. They paid attention to how others asked questions. This could be from other leaders in workplace settings, reading books, or listening to interviews on radio or television. When they heard a great coaching question, they filed it away to use for themselves later.

- The most popular tip was practice. We can talk all day about how to ask questions but until you get out there and do it, you will not get better at it.

Create an environment for asking questions and being curious. Leaders model the behavior for employees. People will listen to what you say, but if your actions don't match, you will lose credibility.

- Reward others for stepping outside their comfort zones.

- Be transparent about your decisions and consistent in your actions.

- Make the time to ask questions and allow others to answer.

- Don't punish others for asking questions.

Don't ask if you don't want the answer. We used to have a leader who would ask the team for input when the decision was already made on how he wanted to proceed. The moment we realized we had spent an hour brainstorming options to make us think he wanted our ideas actually turned into a team bonding experience. Unfortunately, it was bonding us against our leader. If you already know what needs to happen, if things need to be done a specific way and there is no flexibility, or you know your team does not have the information to be able to provide input, then don't ask for their ideas. You will only frustrate them.

Example

I worked for a leader who was great at asking questions in all situations. She had taken the time to build trust between us, so I did not question her intention when her curiosity kicked in. There would be times when I would call her because I was not sure how to proceed with supporting a business partner. Instead of telling me what to do, she would ask me things:

- *What have you done in situations like these in the past?*
- *What is your gut telling you?*
- *What are your ideas?*
- *What are your concerns?*
- *How would you like to proceed?*

We would talk through it, and I felt confident and empowered afterward. Sometimes, I would call her with a problem that was uncharted territory. It had never happened before, so there was not a precedent. Again, she would partner with me by asking questions to figure out what to do. By supporting me in resolving the issue, I felt that she valued me and believed in me.

—Coach Debby

Reflection Questions

What gets in your way of asking questions?

_____

_____

How can you make asking questions a habit?

_____

_____

What are some of your favorite questions to ask?

_____

_____

What is your coaching or communication style (pace, focus, etc.)?

_____

_____

What are some things you can do to keep working on your questioning skills?

_____

_____

Consider an upcoming meeting you have. What are some questions you might be able to ask?

_____

_____

How can you create an environment that encourages everyone to ask questions and be curious?

_____

_____

Capture additional thoughts and big ideas in the journal section in the back of this book.

Other related words: Culture, Curiosity, Environment, Intention, Listen, Relationships, Resistance, Safety, Silence, Trust

RELATIONSHIPS

The way in which two people or groups feel and behave toward each other

—Collins Dictionary

As we write this book, the world is experiencing a health crisis that has created uncertainty and fear. Businesses are having to work differently and make hard decisions. Leaders are being asked to step up in ways they haven't had to before, and some are struggling. They are getting caught up in reports, resorting to micromanaging, and forgetting about nurturing relationships. The sad thing is that we can guarantee that those who are being led are not going to remember meetings and reports, but they will remember how their leader showed up for them—or didn't.

Jim Kouzes and Barry Posner are coauthors of *The Leadership Challenge*, educators, and management consultants. One of their most inspiring quotes is "The best way to lead people into the future is to connect with them deeply in the present. Your focus cannot only be on numbers. You must also focus on relationships. Relationships will help get you to results."[11]

---

11   Kouzes, James M., and Barry Z. Posner. *The Leadership Challenge: How to Make Extraordinary Things Happen in Organizations.* Hoboken, NJ: The Leadership Challenge, 2017.

Too many leaders think their title as the official leader should result in people automatically trusting them. That is not the way human beings work. Your title will not get you good relationships. *You* need to do that. It will be worth it. Relationships will help you build trust, have more influence, and give you more latitude to share a message. (Check out the chapter on messaging if you haven't already.)

What's in it for you? We have learned that having a relationship makes it easier to do things like the following:

- Ask tough questions. When a relationship is in place, people do not feel threatened, there is less chance of them questioning your intentions, and they will remain vulnerable.

- Give feedback. We have found that when people feel safe, they will often share their thoughts and feelings freely. During feedback sessions, they are often harder on themselves than you would be. It sure makes the leader's job easier when the person has self-discovered an issue before we have to say it.

- Understand what is important to someone. This information can help you to motivate them to change a behavior.

- Learn their communication style so you can better communicate with them. Knowing their preferences allows you to be more prepared on how you might need to adjust your communication style with them. It also gives you insight into what they want and need. This includes the best way to support them and challenge them in a conversation.

Don't get us wrong, you still need boundaries. We have seen leaders become so invested in a relationship that they lose their objectivity about the employee's performance, they take on work that should be owned by the employee, and they convince themselves that they need the employee around. Basically, they are being held hostage by that relationship. This doesn't mean that you cannot be social with your team. But you need to be clear where the lines are that you should not cross.

Relationships with your leader and colleagues are just as important as the relationships with your employees. You don't want to forget about those. Leadership will be much harder if you don't have a support network.

Tips

Things can you do to build relationships. This is not an all-inclusive list, but some basics to get you started.

- Listen. When we ask people why they like working for a boss, we often hear, "They really listen to me." Listening is a gift you can give someone, as they are not always listened to in other conversations. It shows that you respect them and value what they have to say.

- Acknowledge. If someone is doing a good job, tell them! Leaders often think that people know when they are doing well and there's no need to recognize their efforts. Studies have shown that if you want to see more great results make sure you are acknowledging their good work.

- Inquire. How are they doing? How was their vacation? What did they think of the game last night? Don't always make it about work.

- Pay attention. You can learn a lot about someone by being attentive. Look at pictures on their desk. What books are on their shelf? What do they talk about a lot?

Do it your way. There is no set way to build relationships. What we do know is if you try to be someone else, it won't work. Figure out what works for you and what you are comfortable doing.

It is a two-way street. You cannot expect others to be vulnerable all the time if you are not. Admitting that you don't know something or sharing a mistake lets people know you are human.

Create a safe space. The Oxford Dictionary defines a safe space as "a place or environment in which a person or category of people can feel confident that they will not be exposed to discrimination, criticism, harassment or any other emotional or physical harm." Have you created a space where your team can ask questions, take risks, make mistakes, and be themselves without fear that there will be reprimands, negative evaluations, and harassment?

Establish mutual respect. How hard would you work for someone who doesn't respect you? It isn't about liking each other. Mutual respect is the recognition that two or more individuals have valuable contributions to make in a relationship. It can be built by being inclusive, considering the impact of words and actions on others, being intentional with your communications, and not getting caught up in gossiping and complaining.

Example

I am a feeler. You have me hooked when you ask me questions about how I am feeling or how others are feeling. Therefore, my focus is often on people. In one conversation I was asking a lot of questions about how the person was feeling about things, because that's what I'd like to be asked. I noticed that they were disengaged, and we certainly were not making progress. Then I asked myself, Who is this person? *I realized that he was analytical, very strategic, and focused on results. I switched my questions from "how do you feel" to "what do you think." He regained interest in our conversation. As my questions became more focused and result-oriented, the conversation became more robust.*

—Coach Debby

Reflection Questions

What are the boundaries you want to set for employee relationships?

_____

_____

What can you do to enhance your relationships with your team?

_____

_____

What can you do to enhance your relationships with your leader and colleagues?

_____

_____

On a scale of 1 (Needs a lot of work) to 10 (Rocking this out), how would you rate yourself on the following:

- Creating a safe space for your team   _____

- Building mutual respect with your team   _____

- Building mutual respect with your leader and colleagues   _____

For another perspective, ask your team or colleagues to rate you on these areas.

_____

_____

What can you do to improve those ratings, if desired?

_____

_____

Capture additional thoughts and big ideas in the journal section in the back of this book.

Other related words: Acknowledge, Emotions, Feedback, Habit, Intention, Language, Listen, Safety, Trust

RESISTANCE

To refuse to accept or be changed by something

—CAMBRIDGE DICTIONARY

WHEN COACHING PEOPLE, sometimes, you will be met with resistance. Resistance is different than not being able to do something, or just not getting it done. Resistance is an intentional refusal to accept something or change a behavior.

When you are working with an employee and the person does not give any indication that they want to change their behavior, this can be considered resistance. In his book *The Power of Habit*, Charles Duhigg states, "People continue behaviors because at some level they get a reward from that behavior." When you are coaching a person and they are resisting change, you have to coach them on their resistance to the change before you can coach them on practicing the desired work behavior.

When a person seems to be resisting, we often check these sources to see how we can help the person overcome their resistance.

- Does the employee lack the desire to do it?

- Does the employee lack the knowledge and skill to do it?

- Does the employee lack the confidence to do it?

- Does the employee have the right incentives for them to do it (or not do it)?

- Does the person understand the importance of doing it?

- Is the employee receiving social/political cues that they should not do it?

- Is the change in conflict with something else they want to do?

- Is the change in conflict because of something they think or believe?

- Is there something about the change that is causing them to be afraid?

After considering these things, schedule some time to talk with the person to determine what is causing their resistance. Don't assume that the first question you ask will result in the real answer. Helping people examine why they are resisting change may be a difficult conversation. Be prepared to uncover many different reasons that the person is resisting change. When the root cause of the resistance is determined, use coaching to help the person develop a plan to overcome their resistance.

As a leader-coach, you can overcome resistance by discovering why it exists and helping your team create new habits. For help with habits, after you read this chapter, see "Habits."

Many times, when people are resisting change, other people assume the person does not know how to do it and they need training. If the person does not have the knowledge or skill they need to complete a task, they need training. If the person could perform the task if they had to do it, then it is not training. The person has some other factor that needs to be addressed that training won't resolve.

When coaching an employee who is resisting change, invest the time to shift their perspective. This can be especially true when trying to change or create new habits. Ask questions that help the employee figure out their triggers and cause the resistance to change. When you ask questions, it opens the person's brain to think about new possibilities. Instead of constantly telling them to stop or start doing something, you ask:

- Why do you think the company is asking you to do this?

- What about the current process is working and what is not working?

- What are the possible outcomes if you don't change?

- What is the best thing that could happen if you do change?

These questions provoke the employee to think about possibilities and not put up defenses.

Get the person to focus on the potential positive impacts of change. Many people fear loss during times of change, and this can cause resistance. Help people work through the fears and apprehension of the changes. When you notice people resisting coaching or resisting change, understand that there can be multiple reasons. Take time and ask questions to help uncover the source of the resistance. Work with the person to develop a plan to overcome the change. Follow up with them to assess their progress and offer support if needed. Use your coaching skills to help the person work through their resistance and embrace the new benefits of adopting the new behaviors to reach the desired outcomes of the change.

There is another aspect of resistance that you may encounter. Some people will resist being coached. The person may avoid interacting with you because they know you will ask the tough questions. People may cancel or postpone meetings because they have not completed the actions they committed to during a previous coaching conversation. There will be some people who will not like the level of accountability that comes with coaching. To help people overcome this type of resistance may require additional time and energy on your part. The first things to do are establish trust with the person and make your intentions for coaching clear. This could be done by having non-coaching interaction where you get to know the person, talk about their interests, and share your intent to help them be successful.

Investing time in building your relationship with the person and creating safety is important. They will base their trust on the words you say, your actions, and the depth of your relationship. As you spend time developing the relationship, help the person understand that your intentions are to move them forward in a direction that is mutually beneficial. The person may perceive the coaching and acceptance of change as only benefiting the company. Let the person know you are coaching them because you are interested in supporting them. For additional considerations, you can refer to the chapters on "Relationships" and "Mindsets."

Tips

Ask thought-provoking questions. When helping a person work through resistance, ask them thought-provoking questions; instead of trying to get them to change their minds. Don't make the person feel like they are a bad person if they are not changing. They may have a legitimate reason for their behavior. Help them examine why they may be resisting and what is holding them back. Consider they may be afraid or fearful about something.

- Ask them about barriers.
- Ask them what their biggest concern is about making this change.
- What seems to be your biggest barrier to success?
- Is what you're doing now working to get you to where you want to be?

- What do you need to be successful?
- What would make this situation better for you?

Share insights with them. Give them a message (you can find more information in the chapter on messaging). Ask them, "What would you do if you knew you could not fail?"

Look for positive role models. Identify people who have the desired attitudes and work behavior, consider people who are earlier adopters to the change and identify best practices they are using. Share those best practices with others who are not adopting or even resisting the new behaviors.

Leverage your listening skills. When people are resisting changes, this is a time for you to really listen to them when you ask them questions.

Become an environmental scanner. When people are resisting become more observant about other things that may be going on in the environment. Look for other factors that may be influencing people or creating barriers to change (i.e., conflicting rewards, office politics or interpersonal conflict).

Give an opportunity for growth. Allow time and space for people to make mistakes.

Example

Sometimes, people don't understand the why of a change or the impact of their behavior. In one of my prior jobs, I had good relationships with people in the IT support group. When I needed help with a tech question, I just picked up the phone and called a friend. One day when I made a support call, my friend asked me if I could submit an online request for technical help. My first thought was Does she really want me to create a work ticket and submit a help request for my problem?

She explained to me that the way her work was tracked and allocated was by help tickets. And her performance was partially based on how she managed her support tickets. She helped me understand that my behavior of making personal tech support requests by phone was causing her work to not be accurately documented. She was doing work that she had no evidence to document she did it.

I honestly had not understood the why behind following the process of submitting help tickets. My behavior changed when I understood and the impact it was having on my friend.

—Coach Kevin

When you believe a person is resisting change, maybe they are questioning your motives. If they are resisting an organizational change, they may be questioning the motives of the organization. Maybe they don't understand the reason why behind the change. Ask the person if they feel like they are resisting and then open the conversation up to why. Having an open discussion with a person about the perception they are resisting organizational changes can lead to understanding and, eventually, acceptance of change.

Reflection Questions

On a scale of 1–10, how would you rate your ability to help people overcome resistance? _____

_____

_____

What steps can you take to improve your ability to coach and lead people through change?

_____

_____

When you notice a person resisting, what is your first thought about them?

- If the thoughts are less than positive (negative or skeptical), how can you evaluate those thoughts to see if they are accurate?

_____

_____

- How do you work with the realities of your thoughts/feeling, the person and the situation?

_____

_____

When you are resisting change or slow to change, what are your reasons?

_____

_____

What is the change methodology on your team or in your organization?

_____

_____

How can you share this methodology with your team and create an environment where people have more change agility?

_____

_____

If the person is afraid of something, how will you express empathy and help them resolve their fear?

_____

_____

Capture additional thoughts and big ideas in the journal section in the back of the book.

Other related words: Change, Mindset, Culture

SAFETY

The state of being safe; freedom from the occurrence or risk of injury, danger, or loss

—DICTIONARY.COM

FOR PEOPLE TO be able to engage in the workplace, they need a certain level of safety. In the past, the focus was on physical safety. People wanted to know that their workplace was safe from physical harm. As we continue in the information age, more people work with ideas and produce conceptual work products. There is an additional level of safety we need to consider and create. We need to create workplaces that are intellectually and emotionally safe. This type of safety is interpersonal safety. People often equate their safety to the level of trust they feel when interacting with you or anyone in the organization.

How safe is it to talk to you? When people talk with you, how do they feel before, during, and after the conversation? It is up to you to create the right climate for the discussion. You can create a safe environment where everyone in the conversation can be open, honest, and considerate. We encourage you to make the person included not feel bad or experience negative emotions.

Another element of interpersonal safety is confidentiality. Can people trust that the things they tell you in confidence will remain confidential? The person should be able to have confidence that the things they tell you will (within legal bounds) be kept confidential. They should be able to trust that you will not talk about them or their situation unless there is a legitimate reason to share.

What level of vulnerability can they have with you? Can the person let down their guard and be open and honest with you? Do they have to be on guard with the things they say? Can they express their emotions? Can they respectfully express their true opinions?

Are you emotionally/socially intelligent enough to understand when you should have and show empathy? See the chapter on emotions and emotional intelligence earlier in this book. You don't have to agree with a person to understand them. While coaching, it is important that the employee believes that you understand them. You acknowledge and respect their feelings, situations, and perspectives. People want to be heard and understood.

If you are working with an employee who is struggling with their performance, allow them to share their perspective of their performance. As the leader, you can and should evaluate an employee's performance without it becoming personal. When evaluating performance and giving performance coaching, focus on work behaviors. An employee can be a good person and a poor performer. Don't link the person's performance to your personal opinion of who they are as a person. All performance issues are not because people are lazy and need to work harder. Be careful that you are evaluating the performance and not the person.

When the person is talking, be open to what they have to say. Be willing to let them share their side of the story before you give your opinion on the situation. Can you listen and suspend your judgment? Can you listen objectively for the facts of the situation and not your interpretation or some other person's interpretation of what happened? Can you hear the facts and suspend your story about the facts until you have the complete picture?

Do people sense that you are authentic? To build trust you should be honest with people. Share stories that show you are a real person too. One of the best ways to create interpersonal safety is to be vulnerable and demonstrate you are learning and growing as a professional and a person as well.

When you are coaching, some people may feel like you are trying to control them or that you just want them to do it your way. They may not understand the intentions of your statements or they may not understand the impact/consequences of their action or inaction.

Do you have the ability to be open to other people's ideas and approaches? Understand that people may want to follow a different path. They may think of things differently and want to try different solutions. To build safety, there should be a level of common respect between the coach and the employee. The employee should understand that you have their best interest in mind. The time and investment you are making in them is to move them forward on their path to success.

Don't have a hidden agenda when coaching your employees. Be up front and honest with people. Share the kind truth of their situation. If their job is in jeopardy, let them know it. If it is not in jeopardy, let them know that also. Be transparent with your motives when working with the employee. Don't let them be surprised by something you should have shared with them. If they are going to lose resources, let them know. If they are moving to a different client, let them hear it from you. When you are not transparent about your motives, when people learn the truth, they will feel manipulated.

You are responsible for creating safety around you. Your attitudes and actions determine how much people trust you. Many times, those you lead will adopt your behaviors and expand the amount of safety on your team and in the organization. To create intellectual and emotional security, it will take an investment of genuine time and attention to each person you wish to influence.

Tips

Listen objectively. When you want to increase safety around you, practice your listening skills. Listen for what the person is meaning, not just what they are saying.

Ask thought-provoking questions. Be genuinely curious about what is going on with the person. Then ask your thought-provoking coaching question. Listen for their thought-provoking answers.

Be authentic. Don't put yourself out as the perfect person. Be vulnerable. If appropriate, talk about your strengths and weaknesses. Let the real you show forth. If you are guarded, others may mirror your behavior by keeping their guards up.

Be supportive. When people need help, be helpful. When people need support, be supportive.

Give your time. When someone comes to your office to talk, if you don't have time, offer a better time to meet. Be honest about your availability from a time, intellectual, and emotional standpoint. If now is not a good time for a conversation, say so and arrange for a good time. If it is an emergency for the other person, then you have to be able to set aside your current situation to help resolve the emergency.

Be Present. When you meet with them, be present and give your full attention. Remove any distractions from the environment where you are having the conversation. Schedule the meeting when you can be present and attentive. If the conversation gets interrupted because of an emergency, be respectful of the employee and set up a later time to talk.

Give Second Chances. Be willing to give a person another chance. Working with people will require you to forgive and give people opportunities for recovery. Be the person who coaches people through challenges to successes. Be a coach instead of a cynic or critic.

Ask for Feedback. How can I create more safety for you? Am I currently doing anything that impacts our relationship in a negative way? When we talk or interact, what would you like to stay the same? What could I do more? What could I do less?

Recover when things go wrong. When you have an emotional reaction, go back and analyze what happened. When a little time has passed, if you realize you owe the other person an apology, then apologize. It there was a misunderstanding, take the initiative and get the misunderstanding cleared up.

Example

During my career, I have had numerous meetings with executives. Each executive had a way of managing the power dynamics of the room, whether it was just the two of us or a small group. During some of those meetings with executives, I experienced many different levels of safety. Some executives made you feel like they were doing you a favor by allowing you to come into their offices and meet with them. Some executives took the opportunity to demonstrate they knew more than you and had more organizational power than you.

There were other executives who managed the meeting in ways that created more safety. They forwarded their phones to voice mail, offered you something to drink. They got up from their desks and came to sit in a chair next to you, chatting about your family and participating in the conversation as a collaborator. These executives shifted their behaviors in ways that created more safety.

If you said or did something wrong, they sought to teach instead of scold or blame. If you failed, they looked to examine the process and coached you on ways to be successful. The executive who created the climate of safety usually got more commitment and work out of their people than those who created climates of fear and compliance. They were able to attract and retain high-quality people to their teams and initiatives. Influential leaders who create intellectual and emotional safety don't scold—they offer coaching and advice. They don't blame—they look for processes and system improvements to avoid future mistakes.

—Coach Kevin

Reflection Questions

On a scale of 1 to 10 (with 1 being no safety around you to 10 people feel totally safe around you)

- How much safety do you create around you? _____
- How good are you at recognizing when people don't feel safe around you? _____

Are people avoiding having conversations with you?

_____

_____

Are people afraid to bring you bad news?

_____

_____

What are three things you can do to create more safety around you?

_____

_____

What is the one thing you will do tomorrow to help people feel intellectually and emotionally safe around you?

_____

_____

How can you make it safer for people to interact with you?

_____

_____

Capture additional thoughts and big ideas in the journal section in the back of the book.

Other related words: Culture, Trust, Intention, Presence, Relationships

SILENCE

A period without any sound; complete quiet

—CAMBRIDGE DICTIONARY

WHEN WE THINK about silence, a quote by renowned author and speaker Dr. Wayne Dyer comes to mind. He said that "everything that is created comes out of silence. Thoughts emerge from the nothingness of silence. Words come out of the void. Your very essence emerged from emptiness. All creativity requires some stillness."[12] How powerful is that?

There are really two parts to using silence: how you use it with others and how you use it for yourself. Let's start with how you use it with others.

Silence can allow people to process what we are asking, reflect on what has been shared, and create space for someone to provide more information. If your intent is for self-discovery, innovation, and getting results, then using silence is a great tool for a leader. Remember, silence is part of listening and being present. You are shifting from solving their problems, to empowering them to solve their own

---

12   "Embracing Silence" on drwaynedyer.com.

problems. Using silence after you make a point, ask a question, or deliver a message, is a leader's version of a mic drop.

What holds leaders back from using silence? Silence feels awkward and makes people uncomfortable: including the leader who is being silent. We think we need to fill the space. A few seconds somehow seem like minutes, or maybe even hours. We encourage you to reframe your brain from "I have to fill the silence" to "I am modeling for this person that it's okay to sit and be silent if that's what they need." Everyone can benefit from time to think. What better gift to someone than to provide the safety to do just that?

A study at the University of Virginia chronicled in *The Atlantic* looked at how difficult it was for people to entertain themselves with their own thoughts for six to fifteen minutes. Participants were wired and provided the opportunity to shock themselves during the thinking period if desired. Even though they all had a chance to try out the device to see how painful it was, a quarter of the women and two-thirds of the men gave themselves a zap.[13] They preferred electric shocks to being alone with their thoughts. That is how uncomfortable we are with silence. What we don't realize is that we have underestimated the power of silence.

The other piece that leaders don't often think about is how to use silence for their own benefit. This could look different for everyone. We often hear leaders share their routines of journaling, meditation, and deep breathing. Others mention taking a walk, working a puzzle, or pursuing a hobby like cooking, woodworking, or knitting. These activities help them to clear their heads and regain energy to allow them to avoid burnout, maintain focus, and be the best leaders they can be.

---

13   https://www.theatlantic.com/health/archive/2014/07/
people-prefer-electric-shocks-to-being-alone-with-their-thoughts/373936/.

Tips

Trust yourself. Don't rush. What you need to say or do next in a coaching conversation will come to you if you leverage silence to be thoughtful about what you just heard. Also, the person you are talking to will experience more forward momentum if you allow them to do the same with a question you just asked.

You need quiet time too. When a coaching conversation is planned, give yourself some quiet time to clear your head and get ready for the conversation. That could look like taking a quick walk or simply closing your door and taking some deep breaths.

Consider the other person. Introverts can really benefit from silence. They need time to process information. They need time to get what is in their heads out of their mouths. Extroverts may need silence to slow them down and force them to think about what they are saying or what they heard. Everyone can benefit from the silence that allows them to reflect.

Use silence to show empathy. Have you ever been sharing what is going on with you, only to have the other person start telling a story about when that happened to them? And they go on and on. They aren't doing it to be mean. They are simply unaware of what that feels like to others. Sometimes, the best way to show support is to be silent.

Silence can be strategic. Did your mom ever say, "If you don't have anything nice to say, then don't say anything?" This has saved us when we have been angry or frustrated with someone. If we had said something in that moment, it could have destroyed the relationship. Silence allowed us to gain clarity and consider what we really wanted to say, while preserving the relationship.

Develop the skill of being silent. Write yourself a reminder on the top of your notepad. Coach JoAnn likes to write WAIT, which equals *Why Am I Talking*? Set an intention before a meeting or conversation to practice silence.

Example

I once attended a meeting where a senior executive was speaking to a group of front-line leaders who had just found out that major changes had been made to their role and some of them might be asked to switch to a different job. You could feel the anxiety of their uncertainty hanging in the air. They were looking for answers, which frankly this executive did not have yet. He showed incredible courage as he stood in front of them and asked what was on their minds.

After each brave soul spoke, the executive asked, "What else?" and then he was silent. This went on for thirty minutes. There was definitely some squirming in seats and looks of "What is happening here? Does he really want to hear what is on our minds?" He did not look frustrated. He did not look annoyed. He was simply waiting until someone wanted to add to the conversation. With each new comment, the answers to "what else" were deeper, more honest, more emotional. I learned that day that what happens after you ask a question is just as important as the question itself.

—Coach Debby

Reflection Questions

On a scale of 1 (awful at silence) to 10 (the silence master), where do you see yourself today? ____ Where do you want to be? ____
How can you close the gap?

How can you practice silence?

_____

_____

Take time at the end of the day to reflect on how you did with silence. What were the missed opportunities?

_____

_____

What does the use of silence to clear your head look like for you?

_____

_____

Capture additional thoughts and big ideas in the journal section in the back of this book.

Other related words: Listen, Messaging, Questions

TIME

The part of existence that is measured in minutes, days, years, etc., or this process considered as a whole

—Cambridge Dictionary

THE MOST POPULAR excuse we hear from leaders for why they don't coach others is that it takes too much time. We understand that time is a hot commodity for leaders. It never feels like you have enough time to do all the things you either need or want to do. It is important that you remember what is most important and what is going to give you the most return on your time. Writer Leo Christopher said, "There's only one thing more precious than our time and that's who we spend it on." [14] Investing in the people around you *is* the most important part of a leader's role.

How long does a coaching conversation take? The real answer is it depends. It depends on the relationship with the other person, how much trust is in place, the situation, and even how much time you have. We have experienced coaching conversations that took ten minutes and some up to a series of conversations in order to support

---

14 Twitter @Leo_Words, October 12, 2015.

another in reaching a goal. When you start seeing the benefits of coaching, it will all be worth it.

It may take a little longer while you are learning your coaching skills. You will get better at it. In the meantime, here are some ideas that might help:

- Show yourself some grace.

- After a coaching conversation, take time to reflect on how it went. What did you do well, what do you need to work on, and what did you learn about the other person?

- At the end of the day, evaluate how you did with recognizing coaching opportunities. What were missed opportunities?

- Celebrate your wins.

The focus of your time should not be solely on conversations, but on creating a coaching environment—an environment where others are open to feedback, empowered to solve their own problems, and get things done even when the leader is not around; an environment where a leader can ask questions, will acknowledge the people around them, and works hard to provide a judgment-free zone. Creating that environment may take a little more time, especially if it is a grassroots effort and not top-down behavior. We have seen both, and it is completely possible.

Although there are some coaching conversations that can be scheduled, ninety percent of your coaching conversations will be spontaneous and unplanned. It might be someone popping into your office with a question, running into someone in the hallway who mentions an issue they are having, or an unexpected phone call that provides information that needs further exploring.

Open your mind to the possibility that coaching can actually *save you time*. We honestly believe that if you make the investment now in coaching, you will soon reap the benefits of no more lines out of your office with people waiting for you to solve their problems. Work will get done even when you are not there. You will see people exceed your expectations. You will develop people who are leaders, whether they want the official title or not. The time you invest will come back to you later, with an empowered workforce that gets results.

Tips

Invest in yourself too. We have already shared the need to invest in others. It is just as important to invest in yourself. Take time to get better at coaching. Ask for feedback. Practice in safe spaces. Take a coaching class.

Limited on time? We know it can feel distracting when an unplanned coaching opportunity pops up in the moment and you don't have the time to have a full-fledged coaching conversation. Here are a few tips:

- Do what you can to be in the moment so you can really listen to what the other person is sharing with you.

- Offer to continue the conversation later when you have more time.

- Leave them with at least one open-ended question to consider in the meantime.

Start by identifying opportunities for coaching. Do you conduct one-on-one meetings with your direct reports? Do you meet with others after a learning experience, a project ends, they reach a goal, or you receive a customer complaint? These are all great examples of when a coaching conversation would be beneficial.

Coaching is not just for problems. *Coaching is only for problems* is a myth. Catch people doing things well and then ask about it. Do this with your team and with others like your peers and your leader too. What are they doing? What best practices might you be able to identify? How can they keep up that performance level or maybe even elevate it? Make sure you acknowledge the good behavior.

Example

I ran into someone I was mentoring in the breakroom and they told me the big project they had been working on was just completed. I knew that I had a meeting that started in thirty-minutes, and I still needed to get something to drink and get back to my office. I let them know that I had limited time and would be happy to talk longer later. Then I acknowledged their hard work and asked the following few questions:

- *What went well?*
- *What didn't go as well as expected?*
- *What would you do differently next time?*

Another example of coaching when there is not a lot of time:

I arrived for a meeting a few minutes early, and a peer shared an issue they are having and told me they didn't know what to do. The meeting was going to start soon. I asked the following questions that I had learned from Master Coach Cheryl Smith to help them get unstuck:

- *What do you need more of or less of?*
- *What is one thing you are willing to commit to addressing in the next seven days?*
- *What support do you need?*

These are examples of how just a few questions can support someone in moving forward without having a lot of time. You will find that sometimes this is all that person needs to feel empowered to solve their own problem and sometimes there may need to be a follow-up conversation.

—Coach Debby

Reflection Questions

What are the opportunities you have for coaching?

_____

_____

What can you do to put a coaching culture in place?

_____

_____

What is your desired outcome for investing time in coaching?

_____

_____

What can you do to invest in yourself?

_____

_____

Capture additional thoughts and big ideas in the journal section in the back of this book.

Other related words: Culture, Environment, Habit

TRUST

---

*The firm belief in the reliability, truth,
ability or strength of someone*

—Merriam-Webster.com

TRUST IS FOUNDATIONAL to creating a coaching environment. Are you trustworthy? If people do not see you as honest and truthful, a person of integrity, someone who keeps confidentiality, it will be hard for them to trust you, let alone be coached by you. And you can *tell* people to trust you but as we discussed in our relationships chapter without a good relationship trust is harder to build.

When people know that your intentions are to help them, to support them, to develop them, they will be more trusting. The more that they trust you, the less they are concerned about telling you things, asking you questions and asking for help. If you build an environment of trust and confidentiality, you will have people who are confident, productive, and engaged.

If a leader does not have trust with the person being coached, they may experience barriers in coaching conversations. Barriers can be created because of past interactions, if the person being coached does not think the leader has their best interest at heart or the leader has done things in the past that has impacted safety and trust.

The words you use and the actions behind them matter. If a person feels like they are being judged based on your words or actions, they will not want to hear what you have to say and will not let you coach them.

Many leaders think their title or position should result in people automatically trusting them. That is not the way human beings work. A leader shared:

> *I had an employee tell me after a couple months of conversations where I was using a coach approach, that they felt like my questions were designed to entrap them instead of to empower them. They thought I was trying to show them how dumb they were. I found this startling, I was stunned, "Wow, how did we get here?" and "How did I make this person feel like this?" As we continued to dig into that, the reason they were resistant to my coaching was because they were not confident that they could really share any of their challenges with me. There was not enough trust between us for a willingness to share their vulnerability or to be transparent. I immediately began to focus on building more trust with this employee. I worked on building a stronger relationship not only with that employee but with the team. We would discuss in team meetings how to build trust and the importance understanding intentions—ours and others. I asked the team to hold me accountable if I violated their trust as I would hold them accountable.*

Tips

Check yourself. If you are a leader that walks in with a hidden agenda, those agendas can get in the way of not just coaching, but also building the trust that you need to be able to coach someone. No one likes to feel manipulated.

Build relationships. You don't have to be best friends with everyone, but you do need to have a level of mutual respect through building a professional relationship.

Be transparent and vulnerable. We cannot expect others to be transparent and vulnerable if we don't practice it. People need to know that you are willing to share your failures and struggles. This doesn't mean that you tell your whole life story but be willing to tell relevant stories and how you worked through them.

Be a confidence keeper. Unless it breaks the organizational code of ethics, keep what others have shared in confidence to yourself.

Support a culture of trust. Strong and consistent communication, following through on your commitments, and giving your folks a voice are foundational to a culture of trust.

Strengthen virtual relationships. The virtual work environment can sometimes impede building a trusting relationship if you don't put in the work. Often people who are trying to coach virtually have difficulty because they have not laid the foundation for a relationship. Leaders need to think about how they can build those relationships, even though they are in a virtual space. Set standards and protocols that encourage communication and collaboration.

Example

It takes time to build trust. I was working with a leader who was trying to build trust with his new team. He was struggling with one particular team member. The leader shared that this employee definitely had their guard up. He described the conversations as superficial and the employee showed no desire to open up and share anything with the leader about what they liked and didn't like concerning their job. I encouraged the leader to keep having regular meetings with the employee and keep the environment safe and nonjudgmental. To the leader's credit, he didn't give up. His consistency and authenticity paid off and the employee began to open up. The leader said after several sessions, the employee began to realize they could trust him, and it was a safe place where they could really talk. The leader described it "like they flipped the switch." They were then able to set some goals and build an action plan. This leader taught me not to give up too quickly, not to be too judgmental, but to allow the person the time to unfold in a safe and trusting environment.

—Coach JoAnn

Remember that every person has their own definition and experiences when it comes to trust. As the leader, it is your job to create an environment that allows them to trust. You will have different levels of trust with each person. To build trust, consider the following:

- Be aware of the language you are using. This could be sending an unintended message to others. Use neutral language as much as possible.

- Build relationships. What do you know about the people you are coaching? What is important to them? What is their communication style? Knowing this type of information can help in your coaching conversations.

- Make sure your actions match your intentions. For example, if a person has a performance issue, they need to able to trust that you are not going to talk about it publicly. This does not mean you hide it from everyone. If a person was going from one team to another team, be honest with the new leader about what is going on. You do not need to hide your employee's weaknesses, but you only discuss them on a need-to-know basis.

Reflection Questions

What does it look like for you to build trust with someone else?

_____

_____

How can you make sure that you are creating an environment for trust to exist?

_____

_____

What is your plan if trust has been broken by you?

_____

_____

On a scale of a 1–10 with 1 being "needs a lot of work" and 10 being "no work needed," how would you rate yourself on the following:

- Integrity   _____
- Trustworthiness   _____
- Relationship Building   _____

What could you do to increase your ratings?

_____

_____

Capture additional thoughts and big ideas in the journal section in the back of this book.

Other related words: Barriers, Culture, Intentions, Language, Judgment, Environment

THE LAST WORD

My final word for you is—believe. To accomplish or to do big things requires a certain amount of belief. We wrote this book with the belief that we could help leaders be better leaders. Each word that we chose to be in the book was done with you in mind. Collectively, these words have the potential to transform you and those you lead or influence into the best versions of yourselves. Why do we believe that? Because we believe that you already have everything you need to be that person. Our book is a tool that helps you discover what has been there all along—a leader-coach. You are in charge of what you choose to believe. Our hope for you is that you recognize that the most important person who needs to believe in you is yourself. We already believe in you.

—Coach JoAnn

Congratulations on investing in yourself and your development. President John F. Kennedy once said, "Leadership and learning are indispensable to each other." We believe continuous learning is what separates the good leaders from the great leaders. Don't put this book on the shelf. Keep it where you can get to it quickly when you need it or in your eyesight to remind you to conquer another chapter when you make the time to focus on you. The beauty of this book is that you can revisit chapters as your leadership journey changes. Consider how each chapter can ground you or grow you as things change. And when you feel like your development keeps ending up at the bottom of your priority list, remember why you wanted to be a leader and the difference you make in the world. Coaches3 is here for you.

—Coach Debby

Recall the quote from Lao Tzu: "The journey of a thousand miles begins with one step." Thanks for making reading this book one of your many steps in your leadership journey. We are proud of you for making it this far in the book and in your journey of becoming a leader who uses a coaching approach to influencing and leading others. We trust that you found relevant and action-oriented content in this book. We encourage you to use it as a reference from time to time. We hope you share the lessons you learned from this book with others. Now that you have finished the book, it is time for practice. Practice will turn knowledge into skill. Properly applied skill will lead to results. Each result will bring you closer to your goals and dreams. One last question: What is your next step?

—Coach Kevin

REFERENCES

Bradberry, Travis, and Jean Greaves. *Emotional Intelligence 2.0*. San Diego: TalentSmart, 2009.

"Emotional Intelligence." Accessed September 18, 2020. https://www.psychologytoday.com/us/basics/emotional-intelligence.

Hutson, Matthew. "People Prefer Electric Shocks to Being Alone with Their Thoughts." The Atlantic. Atlantic Media Company, July 3, 2014. https://www.theatlantic.com/health/archive/2014/07/people-prefer-electric-shocks-to-being-alone-with-their-thoughts/373936/.

Kouzes, James M., and Barry Z. Posner. *The Leadership Challenge: How to Make Extraordinary Things Happen in Organizations*. Hoboken: The Leadership Challenge, 2017.

Miner, John. *Organizational Behavior 1: Essential Theories of Motivation and Leadership*. New York: Routledge, 2015.

Sarkis, Stephanie Moulton. "6 Amazing Things Carl Rogers Gave Us." Psychology Today. Sussex Publishers, January 8, 2011. https://www.psychologytoday.com/us/blog/here-there-and-everywhere/201101/6-amazing-things-carl-rogers-gave-us.

Bridges, William & Bridges, Susan. *Managing Transitions: Making the Most of Change*. Philadelphia: Da Capo Press, 2009

RESOURCES

When we began to discuss a list of resources, we quickly discovered that it could be pages and pages. To narrow that list down, we decided we would share a few of the resources that we either mentioned in our book or that influenced our thinking about being a leader-coach.

The 7 Habits of Highly Effective People: Powerful Lessons in Personal Change by Stephen R Covey

Emotional Intelligence 2.0 by Travis Bradberry Jean Greaves

Emotional Intelligence: Why It Can Matter More Than IQ by Daniel Goleman

The Power of Habit by Charles Duhigg

Crucial Conversations by Patterson, Grenny, McMillan-Switzer

The Leadership Challenge by James M. Kouzes and Barry Z. Posner

The Question Behind the Question by John G. Miller

"The Word on Coaching" podcasts by Coaches3

JOURNAL

Capture additional thoughts and big ideas

_____

_____

_____

_____

_____

_____

_____

_____

ABOUT THE AUTHORS

Debby Neely is an executive coach and skilled leadership development facilitator. She has experience coaching and training in various environments—from a Fortune 50 to small businesses to nonprofit organizations. Debby is very proud to be a professional certified coach (PCC) with the International Coach Federation. She loves supporting leaders whether they hold an official title or not.

Contact information: debby@neelycoaching.com
www.neelycoaching.com

Kevin Fuselier is a leadership coach and learning strategist. He has experience coaching individuals through career exploration as well as high-potential leaders on communication and influence, and executives on leadership presence. He loves helping people recognize and attain their potential. He believes that we all can be better version of ourselves today than we were yesterday.

Contact information: kevin@kcgcoaching.com
www.kcgcoaching.com

JoAnn Auger lives in Virginia, and you will often find her hiking and exploring the beauty of the Blue Ridge Mountains. She is the very proud mother of Mason (Janna) and April (Paul) and an even prouder NanaJo to Sabine, Atlas, and Evander. She spends her professional time in executive coaching, leadership training, and consulting. JoAnn also serves as a mentor/coach to many young professional women.

Contact information: jauger821@gmail.com

Stay connected with Coaches3 by listening and subscribing to our podcast, *The Word on Coaching*, and following us on Facebook. You will hear the latest ideas about coaching, participate in a community of like-minded coaching leaders, and find valuable resources to support you on your journey to becoming a more effective leader-coach.

We love speaking with individuals and groups about coaching and working with leaders and their teams to improve the communication, coaching and performance of their organizations. If we can ever support you in your efforts, please contact us.

CPSIA information can be obtained
at www.ICGtesting.com
Printed in the USA
BVHW031417230622
640497BV00012B/860

9 781737 643807